Advance Praise for

NAVIGATING THE TIDES OF CHANGE

David LaChapelle puts his finger on those global
environmental, social, and economic problems that,
like a black cloth, seem to drape our world in mourning
and disaster. By approaching problems from multiple
levels of awareness, David reminds us that every little
effort we make toward healing the planet counts.
He weaves a book of hope from the threads of despair.
He ...challenges us to become progressively more
aware of the ways in which all life is interconnected,
and how, as part of that interconnectedness,
we can and do make a difference.

— JOAN BORYSENKO,
author of *A Woman's Journey to God*

"A deep drink from the well of wisdom to
nurture the soul's thirst. I recommend
Navigating the Tides of Change without reservation."

— MICHAEL TOMS Founding President,
New Dimensions Radio and co-author of *True Work*

David LaChapelle is a translator who moves between
the worlds. He has a special gift for making visible
the invisible, and for articulating emerging patterns.
A soul poet, storyteller, and provocateur,
David challenges people to live according to their
highest calling — to express their "soul signature"
for the benefit of us all.

— TAMI SIMON, founder and owner of Sounds True

Few books about the complex and confusing
changes facing us have been more deeply felt than
Navigating the Tides of Change. David La Chapelle's
impressive insight comes from an unflinching
look at both the deeper patterns of our planet and
those of the deepest recesses of our souls.

He roams bravely and from the heart, exploring
the relationships among such diverse areas of inquiry
as ecology, mystical experience, and the wisdom of
both indigenous peoples and the scientific enterprise.
Simply put, his gift to us is to suggest inspired
solutions to the personal and planetary problems that
currently grip us, and to motivate us to respond
practically to these dilemmas.

David's personal journey underlies the book's

truths, and the suffering, joy, and spiritual awareness

that undergird his writings are uniquely thrilling.

He shows us how we can nurture the natural world

and participate as citizens of eternity in the

unseen worlds of our sacred wisdom traditions.

We need to put *Navigating the Tides of Change*

on America's list of required readings.

— CHARLES A. GARFIELD, Founder,

Shanti and Shanti National Training Institute, and

Clinical Professor of Psychology University of California

Medical Center, San Francisco

"David is the perfect guide to lead us into these gentle

stories and teachings about our sacred green planet.

With great courage, perfect prose, and deep love,

he guides us into both the devastation and beauty

of our planetary home, asking us to become wise again.

I am grateful that the planet chose David to be our guide,

and that he responded with such clarity, courage, and grace."

— MARGARET WHEATLEY, author, *Leadership and the*

New Science, co-author, *A Simpler Way*

NAVIGATING THE TIDES OF CHANGE

NAVIGATING
THE TIDES
OF CHANGE

STORIES FROM
SCIENCE, THE SACRED,
AND A WISE PLANET

David La Chapelle

 NEW SOCIETY PUBLISHERS

Cataloguing in Publication Data:
A catalog record for this publication is available from the National Library of Canada.

Cover design by Miriam MacPhail; photograph © 2000 Eyewire.

Printed in Canada on acid-free, partially recycled (20 percent post-consumer) paper using soy-based inks by Transcontinental/Best Book Manufacturers.

New Society Publishers acknowledges the support of the Government of Canada through the Book Publishing Industry Development Program (BPIDP) for our publishing activities, and the assistance of the Province of British Columbia through the British Columbia Arts Council.

BRITISH
COLUMBIA
ARTS COUNCIL
Supported by the Province of British Columbia

Paperback ISBN: 0-86571-424-X

Inquiries regarding requests to reprint all or part of *Navigating the Tides of Change* should be addressed to New Society Publishers at the address below.

To order directly from the publishers, please add $4.00 shipping to the price of the first copy, and $1.00 for each additional copy (plus GST in Canada). Send check or money order to:

New Society Publishers
P.O. Box 189, Gabriola Island, BC V0R 1X0, Canada

New Society Publishers aims to publish books for fundamental social change through nonviolent action. We focus especially on sustainable living, progressive leadership, and educational and parenting resources. Our full list of books can be browsed on the worldwide web at: www.newsociety.com

NEW SOCIETY PUBLISHERS
www.newsociety.com

Contents

Foreword

Joan Borysenko, Ph.D

I FIRST MET DAVID LA CHAPELLE — while I was literally navigating the tides of change — on a cruise ship, where we were both faculty at a seminar on spirituality and healing. The ship was rolling, rocking, and posing a primal choice: resistance or surrender. By resisting the unaccustomed movement, my body became tense, and the disequilibrium produced by my inner ear as it tried valiantly to maintain the status quo gave rise to an uncomfortable experience of nausea and disorientation. My desire to jump ship at the next port was strong, but there were two more days at sea before landfall. Those days provided me with an unbidden opportunity to explore the ways in which the rhythms of my mind and heart could cooperate with or resist the larger rhythms of the sea.

When I stopped trying to hold myself rigid, stopped thinking of the waves as the enemy of equilibrium, a stunning shift occurred. Entering into the rock and roll, welcoming the disorientation as a new orientation, I found myself passing through a mysterious portal: I lost my land legs and found my sea legs; curiosity replaced discomfort; peace washed away anxiety. I walked in a state that felt timeless, where letting go was the only true form of power. While I was in this altered state of consciousness — with both heart and mind open — David La Chapelle entered my life.

It was evening, and the moon was shining on the silvered breast of the sea. David was sitting on a chair on a glitzy stage in a lounge better suited to Frank Sinatra. Exuding a tangible sense of peace and wisdom, David strummed a guitar, using rhythm and music to open the doors of perception so that we could appreciate the story he was telling. He spoke with a wholeness of being that went beyond language. He gifted us, and we were able to hear a primal story of creation as our own story.

There, in the lounge of a modern cruise ship floating on the ancient waters of the Pacific, a group of strangers came into coherence with images and feelings that woke forgotten memories. Through story the world — in all its splendor and pain — felt sacred again. To paraphrase a teaching of French paleontologist and Jesuit, Teilhard de Chardin, we remembered that we are spiritual beings having a human experience, rather than human beings aspiring to a spiritual experience. For that brief time, it seemed that all was right with the world.

I fell in love with David that night — with his good heart, bright mind, and remarkable ability to bridge the worlds. He is a prophet for our times, schooled in the wisdom of the wilderness and its timeless teachings, in the wisdom of elders from diverse spiritual traditions who have counted him among their own, and in the wisdom of an intellect always questing for knowledge.

As I savored this extraordinary book that you now hold in your hands, I felt inspired in the true sense of the word: a greater harmony seemed to breathe into me and through me, gently calling me forth from the weary world of care and worry and into the arms of divine belonging. David puts his finger on those global environmental, social, and economic problems that, like a black cloth, seem to drape our world in mourning and disaster. By approaching problems from multiple levels of awareness, David reminds us that every little effort we make toward healing the planet counts. He weaves a book of hope from the threads of despair. He writes about invariant constants — polestars that remain constant even as the world shifts around us — and he challenges us to become progressively more aware of the ways in which all life is interconnected and, how, as part of that interconnectedness, we can and do make a difference. Every challenge, every change, is an opportunity for us to plumb deeply that which is true and good. From this inner well of love and meaning we derive the strength to make necessary changes and the courage, when appropriate, to let go and let this surprising universe recreate itself.

The *Interludes* between chapters are magical stories that speak to the soul. As I read, I "became" the salmon swimming for untold miles through wild seas to come home to the place of my birth in the cold, clear rivers of my ancestral lands; the same life force that spoke to the salmon spoke to me. I "became" Harriet Tubman, risking my life over and over again to take slaves into freedom. I "became" every slave until I was finally at one with the will to freedom — the rogue wave of evolution that crashes suddenly through all limitations and remakes the world.

In every *Interlude* I was reminded of David's navigational metaphor of the polestar — the invariant constant that beams its homing signal over any distance. I found myself dreaming on it, moving toward it, falling into it propelled by the inescapable force of gravity. "What guides me? What is the force of evolution that creates meaning even in chaos?" My heart whispered the truth of David's message, "Love, only love." Every story, every word, every wondrous excursion into scientific theory here in these pages, brought me back to that one polestar.

Love as a polestar might seem a simple message. It is. And it is the invariant truth around which every spiritual system orbits. Love is the strange attractor of evolution, the pulse of the universe. Yet, for many of us, it seems hidden or unattainable. Our disconnection from love is a physical arrhythmia, a disturbance in the natural ebb and flow of cyclical processes in the bodymind. We move so fast that we get out of rhythm. Love is always beaming its signal, but most of us are resonating at too fast a frequency to pick it up. So love, in its tender mercy, reaches through the chaos of our lives through beauty.

This book is a study in beauty. Just when your intellect is chewing on the delicacies of strange attractors and chaos theory, it is swept off its moorings by another exquisite tide. The beauty of David's words as a poet makes his prose among the most memorable you will ever read. The beauty of the stories told in the *Interludes* mirrors your own inner beauty, through which you receive the gift of the story.

This book can restore rhythm and meaning to your life. As each chapter rolls onto the shore, there is rest — an interlude — before the next chapter rolls in. The music is in the pauses. In the silence of your contemplation, or perhaps in the sacred space of your dreaming, the star of guidance that is always shining will more easily peek out.

Whether you have been drawn to this book because of your concern for the planet, your interest in the science of change, or your commitment to the sacred, in it you have found a wondrous and living spirit that will speak to you always of love — the star that will invariably bring you home.

A Page of Gratitude

THIS BOOK IS THE FRUIT of important and cherished relationships, and I would like to take this opportunity to express my gratitude for their presence in my life. I am grateful to Ruby de Luna, who for years has tended the editing of my words and has performed heroic service in making the flow of my ideas more beautiful on their way out into the world. She has been a fine, steady, and good friend.

Sandra Peters, from early on, has been a generous patron and fine friend and has helped create the conditions necessary for work such as this to emerge. Her generosity on many levels has been crucial.

Randy Compton helped support my investigation into Y2K-related problems, an act that helped catalyze the writing of this book. His friendship through the years has meant much to me, and I still hold dear the image of him crossing the valley to be with the lightning.

Russ and Diane Hullet have given much support for my work over the years. Their sharing has enriched and enlivened my life in many ways. I celebrate the many years we have journeyed together and the many yet to travel.

I am grateful to John Steiner and Margo King for their friendship, unbounded generosity of spirit and substance, and particularly for providing the seed support for this book. They are true net keepers of our times.

Nancy Simpson has shared many of the ups and downs of my journey during the formation and writing of this book. She has been a steadfast and loyal friend. I could not have written this book without her.

Roger and Ginny Jordan's lifetime friendship has been an essential element in the gifting of these ideas and passions to the world. My gratitude goes to Roger for his discerning eye and his willingness to challenge me toward excellence, as well as for the deeply maturing friendship we share. My gratitude goes to Ginny for being a soul sister and a gentle and true friend on all the pathways of my journey. I cannot thank her enough.

This book would not have the integrity it does without the diligent efforts of Audrey Keating, my editor. Much appreciation goes to her for the enormous amount of work and caring she poured into the book. She was a delight to work with and has made this book so much more than I could have done alone. Our relationship was a true synergy of intent and action.

I am grateful for my father's gift of scientific excellence, his passion for the natural world, and for all of the opportunities and quiet guidance he has given me over a lifetime.

I am grateful for my mother's philosophical passion and fierce commitment to the natural world. I am thankful that she has given me the capacity to be a vessel for refined ideas.

Suzanne Fageol entered into the final stages of this book's development, and I am grateful for the many ways of her friendship.

Lastly, I am grateful to Maggie Jacoby, my partner, for her patience in living with a writer's consuming passions. I honor the integrity of her challenges and her capacity to live into the depths of a mystery that we can only be. To live next to the fires of the creative process is not always easy, and her strength is a generous extension of her heart.

A Note on the Voice in this Book

THIS BOOK IS PRIMARILY A STORY about our times; facts and scientific observations are embedded in its unfolding. In evaluating this material, it is important that you listen with 'an ear of the heart.' The facts and science are accurate, but the metaphors and analogies I develop out of them are crafted with a poet's eye. A scientific lens of perception offers poets a certain rigor, and I try to make use of that rigor. Some scientists may be uncomfortable if science is used this way. But I am not a scientist, and this book is not crafted in the crucible of scientific discipline. I am a poet and a weaver of language; the book is spun from that discipline, which requires a different kind of attention and a different use of intention.

Interludes appear between the chapters of the book. They are stories about various historical individuals who can be thought of as early map makers charting the landscape of our journey. An *Additional Resources* section at the end of each chapter lists Internet links and books for those of you who would like to learn more about the concepts, people, and ideas presented in the chapter text.

The *Interludes* are written in a distinct voice; in composing them I have used a great deal of poetic license. The dialogue attributed to the characters in the *Interludes* is of my own imagining and is not to be construed as literal. In some cases I have incorporated the sayings of historical characters into the story, but again, the results are not to be construed as literal. My intent in using this voice is to particularize and make accessible the human dimension of the more conceptual and abstract material presented in the chapters. To that end, I have attempted to recreate some of the qualities of the various individuals who are honored in the *Interludes* by imagining myself into the mood and atmosphere of their times. I often think of the voice that emerges as that of a companion whose presence is constant throughout time. We each have the sense of a continuity of awareness that threads through our days. I have simply tried to put a voice to that continuity.

Introduction

WE ARE CURRENTLY IN A PERIOD of accelerated planetary change. Global weather changes, cultural erosion, disease transmission, increased information density, economic systems in transition, technology, biotechnology, the population explosion, shifting patterns of the family, urban sprawl, and the degradation of the biosphere are some of the waves that are cresting in the sea of change. The main thesis of this book is that accelerated change is pushing us to a new understanding of our role upon the planet.

As we deepen our awareness and understanding of the tides of change, what feels like chaos may actually turn out to be a current that can move us into a more coherent resonance with the fundamental rhythms of life. Our daily lives can be enriched, and solutions to our planetary problems can emerge if we are willing to participate directly in an ongoing inquiry into the unfolding of our worlds — both inner and outer. In the past this process has been approached through spiritual traditions and has been enacted in the bodies and lives of various mystics. Now, however, unless all of us participate in this inquiry we may be in danger of being overrun by our own limitations and blindness as a species. The enormous challenges facing our planet as well as our own personal tests and trials are all grist for the mill. At their center is an invitation: we are invited to deepen into a state of awareness in which the unfolding of the cosmos becomes a palpable experience, and to learn about a new level of coherence and integration.

Tides are an appropriate symbol for change. The shifting of the tides is a daily aspect of transformation that literally appears at

1

my front door. I live on the edge of a channel of water that can have tides as high as 20 feet. Other than the movement of night into day, there is no other shift that alters my environment more. Though this change is astonishing in its enormity — just try to comprehend millions of metric tons of water per hour that need to shift to make such tidal motion possible — the process has a predictability and periodicity that is comforting. Tides are like the heartbeat of the planet, a magnificent fluid exchange felt on the shores of every continent. They are an apt example of cyclical change.

Given the proper frame of reference, nearly every change can be seen as part of a larger cycle or process. Point of view is everything. To a lone oyster on the beach, a tide may seem like a world-changing experience. But from outer space, astronauts have seen tidal changes tracing elegant patterns across the oceans. They have been able to photograph the actual wave crests of the tides: the carrier waves upon which storm waves ride. Tides themselves result from the motion of the moon; it in turn is embedded in a space-time well that is a harmonic of much larger universal fluctuations. There are tides of solar radiation synchronized to the sunspot cycle that may have influenced human affairs for thousands of years. There are tides of cellular processes that sweep through our bodies and are intricately bound to the cycle of day and night. Tides of history sweep whole civilizations away and seed the beginnings of new cultures.

From a local perspective a hurricane or tornado is devastating and exacts a frightening toll on the environment. From a planetary perspective, though, localized storms dissipate solar gain and help to equalize the Earth's energy balance. This may not be a comfort for the victims of the storm, but taking a larger view does offer a sense of meaning for what is happening.

A restoration of a sense of meaning is crucial if we are to successfully navigate the tides of change. Many events occur in the world over which we have little or no control. If we can learn to hear, see, and feel the thread of meaning that ties these events together, we can emerge into a world of meaning and connection which is spiritually nourishing and capable of sustaining us through the most difficult of outer changes.

Learning to see deeper patterns within localized change is essential to the process of spiritual inquiry. Without it spirituality degrades into dangerous fundamentalism. Ultimately the acceleration of global changes is pushing humankind into a reformation of spiritual inquiry — one which will link science, religion, the arts, commerce, medicine, and technology into a new whole. These times are extraordinarily rich with possibility.

Numerous agents of change throughout history have exemplified in their lives the larger process that we as a species are undergoing. Since computers are one of the most powerful instruments of change today, I am going to open with a story about one of the men who helped bring about the binary revolution.

Alan Turing is widely credited with being the man who helped launch the computer revolution. In 1936 he published a paper in which he conceived of a linkage between logical instructions, the action of the mind, and a machine that in principle could be housed in a practical physical form. He proposed a machine that would read a series of symbols on a strip of paper. Turing began to search for the most fundamental level of instruction possible. In essence, he arrived at a blueprint for all modern computers by exploring a logical question of mathematics: is there a method or process that will solve all mathematical problems?

Turing's remarkable paper was in some sense a mere afterthought of a central life dilemma: what is the connection of consciousness to matter? His search for meaning was initiated by the brief but powerful relationship he had with a schoolmate when he was 16. The older boy and he shared a deep love of mathematics and philosophy. For two years the two were inseparable as they explored those wide-ranging fields of thought. Then suddenly his friend died leaving Alan with a crisis of the heart. Turing became consumed with the question of what had happened to his friend's consciousness. In particular, he began to explore the relationship of matter to consciousness, a study that was to lead him into quantum theory and later into theories about the organization of life itself.

Turing's personal crisis became the matrix of a life that ushered in the computer revolution and established the field of morphogenetics. At the end of his life Turing was exploring the very issue which is one of the concerns of this book: how is change possible? He developed a theory of chemical reactions based on reaction and diffusion that became the basis of a whole new science, and was one of the first people to explore non-linear systems in a coherent manner. (Incidentally, he is largely credited for the theoretical work that enabled the Allies to crack the Nazi radio code during World War II.) Turing's search for meaning ultimately changed the face of the world. Just as Turing wove a matrix of inquiry around his friend's death that helped transform our planet, so each of us has an opportunity to make searches and discoveries that can illumine our own understanding.

In the fall of 1998 a tropical typhoon drifted north across the Pacific Ocean and came to rest against the coastal mountains of Alaska near my home. The unusually moist air brought record rains, and a stream that comes down from a steep mountain behind my house suddenly switched channels and threatened our driveway. I called some friends, enlisted my family, and we began to try to divert the stream away from our yard. In the process of fighting the flood I discovered a practical illustration of a theoretical principle: a small amount of work done upstream diverts more water than a much greater amount of effort made lower down. The higher we went up the hillside the more effective our diversion work became. Those discoveries provided the inspiration for this book.

As we deal with rapid change, we must find diversion points as high in the system as possible. Otherwise we end up fighting futile battles and become easily exhausted. I have spent a good part of my life listening to the stories of individuals who are in the midst of some sort of crisis. I have never yet heard a story that was not embedded in a larger context. Stories disassociated from their greater environment tend to become tales of problems and difficulties. When a person's story is connected to a larger field of meaning, those same problems and difficulties become indicators of the deepest truths. The solutions to any of our problems — personal or global — are present if we will summon the heart to look deeply into the issues and listen humbly for instructions.

Additional Resources

INTERNET LINKS

http://earthrise.earhkam.udsc.edu/earthrise/main.html
 EarthRISE is a graphical, easy-to-use, and unique front end to a large and ever-expanding database of images of the Earth from space, including images and text from the last 15 years worth of Shuttle photos.

http://www-class.unl.edu/geo109/tides.htm
 This site has an excellent short description of tides, their causes, and interesting bits of information about them. You can learn, for instance, that amphidromic points are areas in the middle of the oceans in which there are no tides. This occurs because of the complex dynamics of standing waves of tides, and their intersections.

http://www.antdiv.gov.au/resources/more res_atmos.html
 A discussion of atmospheric cooling by the Davis Atmospheric and Space Physics Laboratory.

http://www.turning.org.uk/turning/
 This site, maintained by Andrew Hodges, has a complete survey of Alan Turing's life and is a good primer on many of the key ideas that organized Turing's life. It was voted one of the top 100 websites by *Net* magazine.

BOOKS

Hodges, Andrew. *Alan Turing: The Enigma*. Walker & Co, 2000. ISBN 0802775802

Chapter One

THE TIDES OF CHANGE

THE MOON, REACHING DOWN with her attraction for the Earth, gently shifts the flowing substance of the sea. Waters rise and fall as she circles, endlessly falling toward the planet on the contraction of space and time that is gravity. The moon never lands because she has found an orbit, a niche in which to dance. She falls sideways. The seas rise and subside.

At the margin of an ancient continent a biological act takes place that is to change the face of the Earth. In a sun-warmed tidal pool on an unnamed shore, a tiny multi-cellular organism wriggles its way out of the mud, absorbs atmospheric oxygen, and survives. Life, which up till now has been born of and nourished by the sea, leaps to the land. The emergent organisms adapt, evolve, and differentiate into the variety of creatures that now lives upon the Earth.

The leap of life from the sea to the land happened at the margins, at the edge, at the meeting place of differences. In the tidal margins of Africa, a subtle shift in the diet of land-based primates may have supported the emergence of Homo sapiens. Some scientists believe that an adequate supply of certain fatty acids found in seafood helped stimulate neurological changes in these creatures. Over time, with this new-found nourishment, our distant ancestors may have evolved the brain capacity necessary to make the leap from baboon to man. And tidal pools — those small basins of water teeming with life that periodically return to their more spacious origins — may have been the crucibles that made the leap possible.

Today we humans are at the margins of a new shore. The tides of change are lifting us up, and we must adapt in new ways to the rapid transformation of our inner and outer environments. Like the Aleut people of western Alaska, we need to become expert navigators.

The world of the Aleut was as much sea as land, and they became expert at navigating open-ocean crossings. Able to travel hundreds of miles by sea on their way to the Pribilof Islands, the Aleut evolved a remarkable capacity to read the rhythms of their environment. They developed chants that matched the wave cadence of the open ocean swells. By observing the shift in swell frequency, and with their chants as a reference rhythm, they were able to infer the interference patterns created by the islands. Tuning to the differences in frequency of song and sea, the Aleut found their way across the ocean. We, also, need to find ways to read rhythms as we navigate the shifting currents of our changing world.

The Polynesian people traveled in outrigger canoes across the South Pacific. Like the Aleut they counted the rhythm of wave crests. And they looked for signs of birds, whose flight patterns and species helped establish a proper direction for travel. Our capacity to heed indicators from our whole environment can help us to steer wisely, too.

Nainoa Thompson is a modern-day navigator. He was instrumental in guiding the first modern ocean-going canoe from Hawaii to Tahiti without the aid of any modern devices. The journey became a symbolic and literal re-empowerment of the indigenous Hawaiian people. In resurrecting the ancient modes of navigation, Thompson helped restore a way of knowing that provides an important example for us all.

At one point in the journey, Nainoa and his crew had reached the doldrums, an area of calm near the Equator in which clouds are more usual than clear sky. Without access to the stars and moon, his normal mode of navigation proved nearly impossible. What happened next is best told in his words:

> It was getting very intense and I was extremely tired. I was so exhausted. I turned to the rail and I locked my elbows on the rail and tried to get rest standing up. In doing that, in all this rain and all this cold, I felt this warm sensation and my mind got very clear. And I could feel the moon. I knew the moon was up, but I didn't know where it was because I couldn't see it. But somehow I could tell the direction.

Acting on his awareness of the moon's position he was able to successfully guide the canoe across the doldrums, and the voyage was completed. Nainoa's story shows us how trusting past our usual modes of perception and welcoming new ways of seeing can reveal otherwise hidden forms of guidance. Nainoa goes on to describe the art of navigation:

> Navigation that I've spoken of so far is more external; it's what you see, it's looking at stars, infinite and far away; it's looking at small waves that are very close. Taking this information and making it into knowledge is one thing. Being able to navigate is another. There is a whole other journey that goes on, and that is internal. It's one that tests you to do things you can't do in your normal life. Much of navigation is this internal journey. It's a commitment that comes from, I don't know, some place that is very deep inside. I think from the spirit or soul of those who take this challenge.

Thompson is talking about a connection between the outer and inner cues that helped him navigate. What cues do we need to help us navigate as we move across the changing ocean of our times?

We need a series of reference points. For thousands of years sailors have used the stars to help determine their geographic position as they moved across the seas. Songbirds too use the stars as they make their migration flights across the night skies. The stars by which both men and birds chart their way are known as invariant constants. We can define invariant constants metaphorically as those qualities, processes, and hidden organizing fields that endure throughout all change. They are known as truth, and their discovery is the life task of every human being.

The wisdom traditions of the world have charted some of the invariant constants of human experience. Through generations of exploration and refinement, these spiritual traditions have provided a basic "map of the cosmos" from which human actions have been guided. While these traditions have sometimes been encumbered and even blinded by cultural assumptions and conflicts, we can still draw upon the wisdom of their diverse spiritual expression. These traditions are the elders. Through them the voices of our ancestors can travel with us — if we listen respectfully and carry the depth of their experience at our side.

As we navigate we need to know where we stand in relation to the rest of the universe. The Lakota people say they were given the sacred pipe by White Buffalo Calf Woman to help orient them to the great mystery. In a pipe ceremony a prayer is sent to each of the seven directions to establish a clear relationship to the spirit that moves through all things.

European mariners invented the more mechanical astrolabe to help orient themselves as they sailed strange waters. An astrolabe can read the angle between the horizon and the sun or a fixed star. Using this measurement and an astronomical ephemeris, sailors could compute their latitude with some precision. We too need to find ways to orient ourselves to the uncertain and changing world in which we find ourselves.

Understanding our relationship to time is another essential skill for effective navigation. An industrious watchmaker in England created the instrument that helped sailors determine velocity, distance, and position with greater accuracy. Today a global ring of satellites — using time increments measured in nanoseconds — can help us determine our position anywhere on the planet. Mathematical measurements of time help us navigate efficiently. But our understanding of time is also metaphoric. As we consider the turbulence created by our global problems, we need to consider how the headlong rush of modern life contributes to those problems.

We need not become fearful, however. Turbulent waters themselves are a source of creativity and transformation. As we shall see when we explore aspects of the quantum world, at the heart of matter there is a seething froth of turbulence. Out of this sea of violent change, the entire universe organizes itself into the elegance of a flower and the beauty of a sunset.

Chaos is often the boundary of the possible, the new, and the emergent and appears to be essential to the creation of our world. Rather than trying to control and subdue chaos, we are being invited to surf the waves of change with skill and artfulness.

The key to navigating the storms of turbulence cannot be found in any tool or device. The sum of our relationships will establish the overall health of our vessels and their journeys. Hence, an ethic of care and compassion for others is as fundamental as any other tool as we set out on our travels.

Vision is another essential tool for navigators. It is not by accident that the bridge of most ships is often the highest place on the vessel. When we see clearly we can respond appropriately. Navigators today cannot escape the fact that they, themselves, affect the view. Many ancient wisdom traditions understood this connection. Modern quantum theory has confirmed it as an experimental fact. Who we are, what we think, and how we conduct ourselves affect what we see. The art of navigation, therefore, is also deeply personal. Sometimes we may need to give up cherished beliefs and habits that are interfering with true navigation.

We need maps. A map is a memory of what has been explored, a description of what is known. In the early days of seafaring adventure, European explorers sailed into the unknown unsure whether or not they would fall off the edge of the world. The expansion of their maps was the expansion of their story. The same is true for us.

There are stories that chart the sea of the soul, the heart of the creative process. These are the maps of men and women who saw the world in ways that changed it. They function as descriptions of the known world that, paradoxically, invite us to journey outward and explore the still-unknown.

You may have a vessel and you may have crafted the tools and maps to guide you but, until you have come to understand the sea itself, you will not be able to navigate its tides. The entire cosmos is an ocean of waves rising and falling across the vastness of time and space, and we must understand how waves arise from underlying fields of activity if we are to learn to navigate change.

Fields take many forms. Most of us are familiar with electromagnetic fields. The way in which a magnet aligns iron filings gives visible form to a field of magnetism. On a grander scale gravity itself is a consequence of the warping of the field of space and time by the stars and planets. Light is a good example of a field of wave-like energy that expands out through space from stars. The coalescing of that field into particular points of discrete energy drives photosynthesis, supporting life on this planet — an interaction between a field of energy and matter that transforms sunlight into several billion tons of vegetation a day.

In our human interactions, we also have occasion to experience fields at work. When you walk into a room and suddenly begin to feel ill at ease, you are registering a field phenomenon at work. These intuitive hunches, that often appear as bodily sensations, are a consequence of your interaction with the field of another human being. The structure and source of these human fields are a matter of great debate, but their effect is not. The universe is alive with fields within fields within fields. Their mysterious force lines, which align along principles of physics as well as metaphysics, help condition and inform our world. They make up the cosmic ocean, and we shall return to investigating them later in the book.

In the end, the greatest journeys are made because of the call of the heart. Love of adventure and the affection that Meriwether Lewis had for Thomas Jefferson sustained him through the exploration of a new continent. Chief Joseph's love for his people helped him lead what has been called one of the greatest military retreats in history as he raced toward Canada and freedom. Martin Luther King's love of justice and freedom gave him the courage to face the difficult task of helping to ignite the civil rights movement. William Blake's heart helped him transcend an impoverished environment and create a body of poetry and art that inspires to this day.

Without our heart's imagination to carry us over the waters of change, we will be turned aside by the forces of circumstance and difficulty. It is the vision we hold of the possible that takes us through the trials of the present. I invite you to join in the mysteries of the cosmos, to allow yourself to be inspired by the stars of your distant longing, to risk infusing the moment with the breadth of awe and wonder which comes from contemplating the many dimensions of the world around us. Find a song, search for a star, listen to your heart, and join me as we search for a way through the turbulence of our times.

Notes

See M.J. Harden, *Voices of Wisdom: Hawaiian Elders Speak* (Aka Press, 1999) pp. 221 and 219, respectively, for quotations of Nainoa Thompson.

Additional Resources

INTERNET LINKS

http://hikemaui.com/book.html

http://astrolabes.org/
A general overview of astrolabe principles constructed by James E. Morrison, Janus.

BOOKS

Brown, Joseph, E., ed. *The Sacred Pipe: Black Elk's Account of the Seven Rites of the Oglala Sioux.* University of Oklahoma Press, 1989. Civilization of the American Indian Series, Vol. 36. ISBN: 0806121246

Fools Crow, Thomas E. Mails, and D. Chief Eagle. *Fools Crow.* University of Nebraska Press, 1990. ISBN 0803281749

Shackleton, Ernest Henry. *The Heart of the Antarctic: Being the Story of the British Antarctic Expedition,* 1907-1909. Carroll & Graf, 1999. ISBN 0786706848

Heacox, Kim, and Alexandra Shackleton. *Shackleton: The Antarctic Challenge.* National Geographic Society, 1999. ISBN 0792275365

ERNEST SHACKLETON

Ernest Shackleton has been called the last of the great
European explorers. The story of his journey is as compelling as
any adventure saga. By the power of his will, he was able to
survive the breakup of his ship, long treks across sea ice, isolation
on a frozen island, and the daring crossing — in a single lifeboat
— of the worst seas on the planet. Shackleton's actions are one
of the clearest examples from history of right use of will.

We stood looking down at a distant human being walking the edge of Stromness Bay, our first glimpse of anyone other than ourselves in a year and a half. The whaling station below us was as near to heaven as anything I will ever see on this Earth. All that remained between us and the end of our journey was a short descent.

We cast about for a way down and soon saw to our consternation that the only path off the mountain was through a waterfall. How fitting, I thought to myself, that our journey should end by our having to descend through a waterfall. For water, in one form or another, had been our friend, enemy, guide, persecutor, and savior.

Who would have guessed, as we cast lines from the docks in England, that we would be standing here now? Three ragged figures who haven't bathed in a year and a half, ready to take a final shower in nature's finest and coldest and return to civilization.

That we stand here at all is by the grace of God and the compelling force of Mr. Shackleton's will. It was he who held my shipmates together as we weathered the months of immobility after our good ship *Endurance* was locked in the ice. It was he who lifted our spirits and laid down the discipline that kept us from tearing at each other like hungry dogs. It was he who said, as the pressure ridges of ice finally converged and submerged our ship, "Don't worry, lads, we will make it home."

Another man might have spoken those words and we would not have listened. But when Ernest Shackleton spoke those words, we believed. And he did not let us down. Guiding us through rotting pack ice in the three small lifeboats we saved from our ship, he led us to Elephant Island.

At any time on any of those dangerous days we could have lost hope. It had been hard enough to leave England just as war was declared, hard not knowing what kind of world we would return to. It had been hard enough to wait out the months not knowing if we would be freed to sail again, hard to watch our food dwindle away and to have our feet forever cold. But in three open boats at the mercy of the pack ice? Well, then giving up would have been easy. It only took one look in the eye of Mr. Shackleton to sweep away what doubt we might have had. He did not let us down.

And what of the crossing of the *James Caird*? A small lifeboat with six men crossing the most treacherous body of water on our planet. Never has such a crossing been made in the history of this world.

Take a globe out and hold it in your hand and you will see the problem. To cross from Elephant Island to the South Georgia whale station, we had to cross a sea that has no land to tame it. The winds blow all round the girth of the Earth and have no tether to hold them back. We had eight hundred miles of the worst seas in the world to cross in order to reach any hope of help for our shipmates.

We sat in that poor little boat for days, sipping water we melted from ice we had stored in the boat. It tasted sour with the bilge slop of our small craft. Our thighs rubbed raw from the salt water, and our fingers blistered from frostbite. A wave, larger than any wave should have been, nearly took us down.

Mr. Shackleton said, as we made it through the maelstrom of the wave, that in all his years at sea he had never seen such a wall of water. The soul of that wave must have passed into him because, when we finally landed on South Georgia, he woke us screaming, "Run for your lives, boys!" He had mistaken a cliff wall for a giant wave.

It was a miracle we landed at all. Thirty- and forty-foot waves crashed down against the cliff sides. Reefs grabbed the sea and broke its back against the land. We fought a steady head wind through heavy surf and past icebergs and finally tacked into a small bay. And when we were still a mountain range away from our salvation, it was Mr. Shackleton who compelled us to continue.

What fire he was made of, I do not know. I swear to this day that looking into his eyes during that final journey over the mountain range was like looking into the force of God. Not that I mean he was God. Lord, no, he was as human as the rest of us. But something inside of him connected with something much larger. And that you have to call God.

Mr. Shackleton told me once that he was guided to Antarctica by a dream. "We were beating out to New York from Gibraltar, and I dreamt I was standing on the bridge in mid-Atlantic, looking northward. It was a simple dream. I seemed to vow to myself that some day I would go to the region of ice and snow and go on and on till I came to one of the poles of the Earth, the end of the axis upon which this great round ball turns."

Standing at the edge of our final descent, cold, raw, tired, hungry, weak, delirious, and within sight of salvation, I have to say that all that kept us going was the compelling force of Mr. Shackleton's dream. What else could have gotten us down that waterfall, down that ice field and back to safety? It was not my skill, that I will tell you. I felt like one dead as I dangled on that rope in the final force of the water. The ice-cold fingers whipped my body and stole my strength. Compelled by a dream, driven by something greater than any of us, we staggered off that mountain and into history.

Mr. Shackleton left the next day from the whaling station. It took him several boats and as many tries, but he made it back to Elephant Island and rescued all my shipmates. Not a one of us died, not one, when we should have all gone many times over.

What urged him to lead us beyond ourselves? He understood the answer. He even reached into that Irish soul of his and found words to offer as a benediction. He quoted us Robert Service's *"Call of the Wild:"*

Have you suffered, starved and triumphed,
groveled down, yet grasped at glory,

Grown bigger in the bigness of the whole?

"Done things" just for the doing, letting babblers tell the story,

Seeing through the nice veneer the naked soul?

Have you seen God in His splendors, heard the text that

nature render?

I can still feel the slice of that final waterfall upon my skin. But what I can feel even more strongly is the hand of the greater will that compelled us to succeed.

Chapter Two

LISTENING TO THE VOICE
OF THE WORLD

"IT CAME OUT OF NOWHERE." The Coast Guard midshipman was pointing at the buckled forward plates of his ship as he spoke. "I was on the bridge when it hit. The wave broke over the windows. For a moment, I thought it was going to tip the whole ship. The seas were running ten to fifteen feet, but there was no clue that such a wave could possibly appear so quickly."

The bent metal plates before us were the signature of the force of the wave. I had heard of rogue waves for years but had never met anyone who had seen one until I took a tour of a Coast Guard ship that had docked in my home town. The crewman I spoke with stressed how utterly unexpected the wave was. Rogue waves arise from a confluence of forces whose effects are not visible until they combine to reveal themselves. When the underlying dynamics of the sea create the necessary conditions, wave crests from differing directions coalesce to push the sea up to unimaginable heights. The wave appears to come out of the blue because there is no real clue that it is coming. The changes that are occurring across our planet have a similar capacity to coalesce and create effects far beyond the obvious.

I travel extensively, and throughout my travels in recent years I have heard conversations in airports, taxis, movie lines, and other public places. The conversations are about how much things are changing. It is now virtually impossible to go to any area of the globe and not hear first-hand reports of strange weather. The discussions of change are not limited only to weather, either. I have heard people lamenting the loss of a favorite species of tree or offering a perplexed observation that some areas are overrun by a particular species of animal or insect.

Worldwide, large population bases are directly at risk from environmental declines. From the thinning of the ozone, to the emptying of the aquifers that feed our major food-producing regions, to the collapsing North Atlantic and North Pacific fisheries, alarming environmental change has become ubiquitous. As we consider a few emerging planetary conditions, it would be good to remember the words of my Coast Guard friend. "I would have never guessed the sea could produce an event like that."

A word about listening to difficult tales is in order here. Twenty-five years as a healer, listening to stories of the pain in individual lives, have taught me many important lessons. Perhaps the most important of these is the art of listening. If I reduce the pain I hear to a static moment, if I try and freeze it with my understanding, then I have interrupted a process which always has a deeper meaning embedded within it. Pain is a messenger, a strange winged visitor that asks us to pay attention and listen beyond our usual preoccupations and concerns.

I invite you to listen to the pain of the planet. There is a message on the winds and in the seas, a message that needs to be heard. To push away the pain is to deny the possibility that solutions can be woven through us. We need to listen with compassionate openness and a deep sense of responsibility.

There have been five major species extinctions since complex life evolved on this planet. Scientists estimate the current species extinction rate to be between 40 and 1,000 times the background rate of extinction. (The background rate of extinction — throughout planetary history — is conservatively estimated to be around one to three species a year.) If the current trend holds, then we are indeed living through another major species extinction. One in eight plants worldwide, and one in three in the United States, is under threat. Over half of all primates are in danger. Since 1900, 123 freshwater species of marine life have disappeared, and another 50 percent may be in trouble.[1]

The cause of the sixth extinction, the one we may be witnessing now, is very clear: we are our own enemy. The global catastrophe of our era is us. Humans have introduced changes into the ecosystem that are responsible for the launching of a possible sixth extinction event. The die-off has not yet reached the level of a major extinction event but, left unchecked, current patterns will almost assuredly produce one.

For the past eight years I have been going to a secluded bay south of Juneau for renewal and to reconnect with the natural rhythms of the Earth. When I first started going, each night a multitude of frogs would appear from under the tall stems of the beach grass. As I walked from my tent on a small trail down to the tidal flats, inevitably four or five big frogs would jump out from under my feet. There was even an occasional frog song in the night, a welcome addition to the quiet of the Alaskan wilderness. Several years ago the frogs began to disappear. This last year I saw only one frog and heard only silence as the moon pulled the tides in and out of the bay.

The loss of frogs is not limited to this one bay south of Juneau. Worldwide, they are in steady decline, and there is no clearly understood reason for the drop in their population.[2] A particular kind of skin fungus that interrupts respiratory cycles has been implicated in some mortality rates in Central America. (Most frogs breathe through their skin.) But, aside from this one example, the frog deaths are a mystery.

Amphibians live in air and in water and are continuously testing the condition of both. Thus, they are considered an important marker species of global health. And the results of their tests are not encouraging. Pollution, habitat destruction, increased UV radiation, invasive pathogens, and shifting populations of predators have all been put forward as possible causes of the decline in frog populations. If you trace the sources of these disturbances back, you end up looking at a human being every time.

Here in Alaska there have been several major outbreaks of spruce bark beetle in the state's forests. Large swaths of trees are brown and dying. Over 2.3 million acres of spruce have succumbed, the largest non-human-induced death of trees on the planet. There is no clear connection between the death of the trees and human activity. Or is there? Rapid warming of the Arctic regions may have shortened the reproductive cycle of the spruce beetle from two years to one, allowing it to become much more prolific. Recent research by forestry scientists points to planetary warming as part of a larger cycle of weather change that is inducing tree weakness.

The trees of Alaska are not the only trees succumbing to disease and stress.[3] In California, Ponderosa pines are dying off along the foothills of the Sierras, due to elevated levels of ozone from pollution in the Central Valley. Ponderosa pines are exceptionally sensitive to ozone — it enters the trees through the stomata, bleaching chlorophyll and interrupting photosynthesis. The East and West Coasts have seen a die-off of dogwoods. Red spruce on the East Coast have been hit by disease. Fifty percent of the saguaro cacti near Tucson have died. The sabal palms of Florida are dying in unusually large numbers. The reasons for the decline of these and other tree species are varied. Increased UV radiation from ozone thinning, pollution, human disturbance, and rising sea levels have all been implicated. Epidemics appear to be affecting our forests — epidemics that ultimately disturb the primary filter systems of the planet's atmosphere.

Why should we care if species are dying off? We should care because survival of our food stocks, medicinal plants, and the healthy functioning of the Earth that supports us depend on diversity and balance among all species. Consider what can happen when the balance is tipped.

I first heard about the decline in the Steller's sea lion population in the mid-1990s. At that time I took note and filed the information away for a different day. The first economic ripples were felt as managers of the North Pacific fisheries met and ordered some curtailment of fishing activity in response to the loss of the sea lions. A news item from Unalaska (a town in the Aleutian Islands) announced that benefits for city employees would be cut in anticipation of the loss of revenue from reduced fisheries. Disturbance in the ecosystem rapidly crossed over into economic disturbance for that community. (A similar Steller's sea lion die-off is being reported in Australia, raising the possibility that a global disturbance is contributing to the problem.)[4] But what caused the Steller's sea lion to decline in the first place?[5]

It wasn't until researchers, studying another species in decline, began to publish their findings that the reason for the Steller's sea lion loss came into focus. Sea otters, once hunted to near extinction along the Aleutian chain, have been making a dramatic comeback. That is until the last few years when their numbers sharply dropped, due to predation by killer whales. Killer whales and sea otters have coexisted for centuries. Why, suddenly, had the whales become killers among the otters of the North Pacific? Because their preferred prey, the sea lions, were disappearing. The sea lions, it turns out, were declining because their main foraging fish, species like herring and ocean perch, were also disappearing.

What accounts for the decline in herring and ocean perch? Three hypotheses have been put forward. The first is that overfishing by commercial fleets is disturbing the balance of marine life in the North Pacific. The second is that the warming of the ocean is upsetting the ecology in unpredictable ways. The third is that an increase in the population of pollock — a predator fish — may be tipping the balance. The pollock are thought to be increasing because of an increase in availability of the microscopic animals they use as food — the same microscopic animals that used to be kept in check by the whales.

Where did the whales go? Humans hunted them.

Our planet is in trouble. Consider some further evidence. The thermosphere is the outermost edge of the Earth's atmosphere, and scientists have long predicted it would be affected by global warming. They hypothesize that a rise in atmospheric carbon levels from the burning of fossil fuels traps heat near the Earth and leads to a cooling of the thermosphere.[6] When gases cool they contract and the atmosphere shrinks. In the last 20 to 30 years the thermosphere has shrunk five miles. (How much of a rise in carbon are we talking about? It is estimated that the CO_2 level has risen 29 percent above pre-industrial levels. This is the sharpest spike of CO_2 levels in 160 thousand years. Like the skin of a desiccating fruit, the Earth's atmosphere is contracting around the entire planet.)

In the Rocky Mountains spring has been coming earlier and earlier, and average nighttime temperatures have been rising as well. A species of grass found throughout Colorado has taken advantage of this shift and is proliferating rapidly. It is edging out another drought-resistant grass that is the primary forage for both wild and domestic animals late in the season. The range may lose its capacity to support foraging mammals due to the rise in nighttime temperatures. Suddenly the carbon output of industrial nations is beginning to bother ranchers in western Colorado.

Pack ice in parts of the Arctic Ocean has thinned between 20 and 30 percent. In addition, the margin of the ice has migrated nearly 100 kilometers north. The ice is breaking up earlier and appearing later. So late that this past fall the traditional walrus hunt of Alaskan villagers on the Bering Sea was delayed two months while they waited for the ice to return. Pack ice provides a platform for mating and resting which brings the walrus within hunting range, and the villagers rely on walrus as a mainstay of their subsistence diet and lifestyle. There is widespread concern that if the pack ice retreats away from the continental shelf — a margin that is rapidly being approached — the walrus will no longer return at all.

In 1998 a 2,000-square-kilometer chunk of the West Antarctica ice sheet collapsed. What had before been a large ocean-supported ice field simply fell apart into small chunks. This is considered a strong indicator of global warming since many scientific models predict that during global warming the poles will heat up faster than any other part of the Earth.

Globally, 1998 was the warmest year on record in the history of modern weather-data gathering. The summer of 1998 had an average temperature of 62.06 degrees Fahrenheit — 1.2 degrees Fahrenheit higher than the 1880-1997 mean. From floods in China and hurricanes in the Caribbean, to drought in Texas and fires in Florida, the year was filled with intense weather-related phenomena. The storm track of the winter of 1999 continued the trend. For well over a month, hundreds of thousands of people were without power due to ice storms and snow-related damage. In the spring of 1999, wind speeds in tornadoes in Arkansas exceeded 318 miles per hour. These are the strongest winds ever recorded anywhere. Vectors of disease transmission are changing because of elevated temperatures. Food production and distribution are under stress. Fishing, hunting, and agricultural patterns, as well as the business and other cycles associated with them, are all shifting in reaction to these changes.

We live on an interconnected planet. Weather and food, planetary ecosystems and human economies are woven together. Make a tear in one place and you damage the entire cloak. (It is a maxim of whole systems theory that local trends can have global repercussions.) Much argument can be made about the causes of global change, and bewildering statistics can be assembled on all sides of the debate. It's hard to know what to believe. So let me ask you this simple question: Is your childhood home in better ecological shape now than when you grew up? I'd be willing to guess that for most people the answer is No.

What can we do? How do we respond? Our nervous systems were designed for life in a hunter-gatherer culture. As agriculture began to take hold our need to organize, store, and communicate information gave rise to the first writing and mathematical processes — an impulse that has intensified ever since. Now we are being asked to integrate vast amounts of data and make an accurate appraisal upon which the survival of our ecosystem depends.

As we try to make sense out of our rapidly changing world, it is far too easy to go to sleep — either literally or metaphorically. Learned helplessness is a psychological process that occurs when stimulation oversteps our capacity to integrate input from our environment. We give up trying to learn or change because the stress of our world is greater than we can process.

If we are to answer the crucial questions that face us, we need to stay awake. Telling stories is one way of staying awake. Paradoxically, when we enter a story, we relax and screen out extraneous input. Information is organized by the act of storytelling into meaningful, coherent, and often mesmerizing patterns. I will be telling many stories in the hope that you will be inspired to stay awake.

What else can we do? Become more aware of the situation. Most of the serious environmental damage being done on the planet is the result of decisions made with a limited view of the consequences. We cannot hope to know the entire picture. But all those who make the effort to educate themselves about global change will contribute to a more positive outcome.

I live in the Tongass National Forest. Federal land starts just behind my home. When I first came to Alaska ten years ago, two pulp mills were harvesting millions of board feet of timber under federal subsidies that were costing taxpayers millions of dollars per year. Aside from being economically unsustainable, the clear-cuts were environmentally damaging. Today, both those pulp mills are closed, and the timber harvesting practices of the Tongass are slowly coming back to a more reasonable and sustainable level.

Many factors conspired, in the face of great odds, to help restore some measure of balance to the Tongass. But probably the most important single factor was a shift in public attitude toward the environment. Awareness led to coordinated action that resulted in specific and measurable change. Never underestimate the capacity of awareness to bring about change. What we do counts. Every action, every day, builds toward certain outcomes.

Positive environmental activities are already taking place in many parts of the world. Increased efficiency in machinery, building insulation, and other technological functions has led to a more efficient use of oil — slowing consumption of finite fossil fuels and buying time for the development of alternative energy sources. By taxing companies based on their true environmental costs, some countries in Europe have begun to create ingenious systems in which the waste products and heat of one industry are recycled immediately into other useful products or processes. There is much we can do and plenty of information available that can help us initiate the actions that need to be taken.

It is possible to listen to the Earth — directly, immediately, and concretely. It means paying attention to the subtle clues our bodies give. It means staying awake to our dreams. And it means dropping our preoccupation with incessant scripts of worry and negative self-talk.

I challenge you to be scrupulously honest in your research. Go to areas of undisturbed beauty. Go to the clearcuts, rock quarries, and polluted waterways. See how you feel in each. Your feelings may have more impact on you than any amount of reading and studying.

We are exquisitely sensitive organisms. We have the capacity to sense and react to our environment on very subtle levels. And we have the unique capacity to translate our sensitivity into words, images, and thoughts. Dare to be an artist for the Earth. Dare to say what it is you feel. This demonstration of courage will help keep you steady as you survey the waves of change washing over our world.

It is important to remember that the cosmos acts more like a song than an impersonal mechanism. Sound recordings have been made of the solar wind as it acts upon the magnetosphere of Earth's atmosphere. (Visualize a soap bubble being gently deformed by the breath of solar radiation.) The voice of the solar wind — aptly named "chorus" — is both ethereal and haunting. You can hear echoes of crickets and snatches of whale song in this celestial, starry music that bathes our planet. Everything is in vibratory relationship with everything else. From the "strings" that may underlie all matter, to the fluctuating pulses of cosmic radiation that attend the expansion of the universe, there is a song that sounds through the fabric of our physical universe. The music of life is heard everywhere. It is we who choose, in the narrowness of our attention and fixation on our own concerns, to fail to hear the music.

Notes

1. See http://physics.www.edu:8082/jstewart/scied397/brian.html for information on species extinction.

2. See http://www.nbii.gov/issues/frogweb for information on the decline of amphibians. This is a United States Government site.

3. See Charles E. Little, *The Dying of the Tree: The Pandemic in America's Forests* (Viking Press, 1995).

4. See http://www.enn.com/news/enn-stories/2000/03/03032000/aslion _10647.asp for information on the decline of the Australian Steller's sea lion population.

5. See http://www.sfos.uaf.edu/msl111/notes/steller.html for information on the Steller's sea lion. This site originates from the University of Fairbanks School of Fisheries and Ocean Sciences.

6. See http://cdiac.esd.ornl.gov/pns/current_ghg.html for a well-documented site on CO_2 levels. See also http://www.ecobridge.org/content/ gevd.htm.

Additional Resources

INTERNET LINKS

http://www.well.com/user/davidu/extinction.html#anchor18171
This site has numerous links to studies that document the rapid decline of many plant and animal species.

http://www.earthjustice.org/work/stelhome.htm
Note: It is "msl" (the letter, not the number one). University of Alaska Fairbanks fact page on Steller's sea lions.

BOOKS

Brown, Lester R. *State of the World 1998: A Worldwatch Institute Report on Progress Toward a Sustainable Society.* W.W. Norton & Co., 1998. ISBN 0393317277

Leakey, Richard and Roger Lewin. *The Sixth Extinction: Paterns of Life and the Future of Humankind.* Anchor Books, 1996. ISBN 0385468091 An excellent work on biodiversity by the paleo-anthropologist and Director of the Kenyan Wildlife Service, Richard Leakey. Leakey sums up many theories of evolution, survival, and extinction and gives some of his own.

Oelschlaeger, Max. *The Idea of Wilderness: From Prehistory to the Age of Ecology.* Yale University Press, 1993. ISBN 0300053703 This book traces the development of the attitudes and interactions that humans have about and with nature. The author is a Professor of Philosophy and Religious Studies at the University of North Texas. It shows; the book is thorough and rich in ideas, detail, and insight. I have read parts of it and found it fascinating but heavy going.

Raup, David M. *Extinction: Bad Genes or Bad Luck?* W.W. Norton & Co., 1992. ISBN 0393309274

Wilson, Edward O. *The Diversity of Life.* W.W. Norton & Co., 1999. ISBN 0393319407 This is a great book! Lyrical as well as scientifically thorough without being tediously technical. A wonderfully written, incisive primer on biodiversity and the functioning of ecosystems and evolution. (Wilson is a winner of two Pulitzer Prizes.)

SALMON

*The salmon's instinct to return to home waters after their
long ocean journey is one of the heartbeats of the Earth.
Finding home is important to us, too. Each of us has a
responsibility to find that stable, known sense of self to which
we can return again and again.*

The wind surges were gentle where they swam. A delicate
hand seemed to tug at their scales and that was all. Light
on the surface was a distant glow; the darkness below, fathoms
in the making. How long they had been swimming, not one of
them knew. The salt of the ocean had long since worked its
changes in their gills, and the sweet water of their home river
was a distant memory. Silver-sided and sinewy, they swam far
into the currents of the calling sea until the urgency of their
journey exhausted itself.

In the semi-darkness of the depths a shift in their bellies
announced a change, and it was time to return home. The
fingers of the sea, the textures of its many waters, flushed
through their gills and bathed their bodies. No shoreline could
guide them, no starlight, no sea floor. Nothing but vast shifting columns of water ... water that translated the touch of the

moon, the spin of the planet, and the warmth of the sun into motion ... motion that rocked them from all directions ... motion that wrapped them in thousands of ways.

The first few molecules were enough. A smell of something that had once meant home lingered in the touch of the sea ... a dilution of a glacier-fed stream ... only a couple of signatures in an ocean composed of billions upon billions upon billions of molecules. The minute remains of a river that had once reflected eagles and eddied around spruce roots washed against their silvered bodies ... aroused an urge to seed new life in water that was shallow and sweet. They were still far, far from shore, but they could smell the water of their birth ... and it was enough ... a molecule or two in a surging column of water rocked by gravity into the weight of mountains in motion was enough .... The salmon were returning home ... and nothing could stop them.

Chapter Three

SECRECY, THE BUDDHA, AND THE VEIL OF UNKNOWING

IN 1629 A DUTCH SHIP is caught in a storm off the coast of Australia. The ship soon founders and the captain and crew are forced to make for shore. The small group of storm-weary sailors find themselves in a strange and exotic land. While they wait for rescue, they explore the landscape of their temporary home.

The sailors see large creatures that hop about on their hind legs. They see birds as tall as men that seem to hide their heads in the sand and furry bear-like creatures that live in trees. But by far the most bizarre animal they see is a furbearing creature that has webbed feet and a bill like a duck, sharp spurs like a rooster, and a flat beaverlike tail. The creature lays eggs like a reptile and yet nurses its young with milk like a mammal.

The diligent captain duly reports these discoveries in his ship's log. The sailors are eventually rescued and taken back to their homeland where the captain is questioned about the fantastic creatures he has described. Scientists of his day concede the possibility of the kangaroo, the ostrich, and the koala, but they balk at the platypus. "Impossible," they say. "No such creature could exist." The captain's descriptions are dismissed as the uneducated observations of a sailor clearly not trained to render exact descriptions of wildlife.

The platypus continues to live unmolested — despite its official nonexistence — for another 100 years. Then an Australian settler catches one and sends its skin to scientists at the British Museum in London, who pronounce it a fake. (That skin is still at the museum, and you can see the scissors marks where they attempted to detach the bill to prove their point.) One hundred-and-sixty more years pass before a researcher sails to Australia and studies the shy animal in the wild, after which humans finally pronounce the platypus an official creature.

What we see is culturally and socially constructed. The platypus was "an impossible creature" because scientific constructs of the seventeenth and eighteenth centuries had nothing in them that could account for its existence. Lest we dismiss those constructs as naïve, thinking that such a thing could not happen in this day and age, consider the story of the *USS Juneau*.

In November 1942, after a night of fierce fighting in the South Pacific, the crew of the damaged *USS Juneau* are busy repairing their vessel. A lurking Japanese submarine manages to release two torpedoes before fleeing; both find their mark, sending the *USS Juneau* beneath the waves. Nearby American vessels steam out of harm's way, unaware that more than a hundred men have survived the disaster. Not wanting to break radio silence, the commander of the retreating flotilla does not broadcast an appeal for help. The survivors make their way through water blackened with bilge oil and into three inflatable life rafts. Wounded, oil smeared, and in shock, they wait to be rescued.

But it is as if the silence and secrecy imposed by the commander somehow suppresses people's awareness of the existence of survivors; though they are spotted several times by crews on surveillance flights, no message is passed up the chain of command. By the time someone in a rescue plane notices them, only a few of the men are still alive.

The sinking of the *USS Juneau* made headlines not so much for the botched rescue effort as for the death of the five Sullivan brothers. The deaths of all five from the same family at the same time became an icon of loss for the nation. What the nation was not to know was that many more died because of the distortion in perception created by military protocol. Once secrecy became the lens of perception, lives were sacrificed in order to sustain the illusion.

In the case of the *USS Juneau* what people saw — or rather what they didn't see — was constructed by habituation and adherence to military protocol. No one had been told to expect to see survivors, so in some sense at least, they didn't see them.

We, too, wear blinders that limit and blind us to the realities of our global situation. A subtle veil occludes our vision. It is woven from threads of belief — belief in systems and technologies that tantalizingly promise solutions if we will only move more information faster and deliver more services more quickly. Seen through the veil, damage to our world is seen as isolated problems to be contained rather than as an index of underlying dysfunction to be healed. Seen through the veil, the true extent of our global problems can be swept under the carpet of business as usual.

The Buddha discovered several thousand years ago that reality (within the world or within us) is created through relationships and that his internal condition was dependent on external events. This is not a difficult concept to understand when we relate it to the physical world: our bodies heat up when we sit in sunlight because they absorb radiant energy from the sun. When rain falls, rivers rise. When you step on the gas, your car speeds up. The concept is a little harder to grasp when we relate it to our feelings, thoughts, and reactions, but it holds.

If you follow a feeling to its origins you will see that it arises in response to a web of connected events that exist beyond your own body and mind. If you are angry with your son for watching TV instead of helping around the house, investigate the source of your anger. You may find that the barometric pressure has influenced your endocrine system and is altering the intensity of your emotional response. You may be resenting the influence TV has on your son's life or the amount of sugar in his food that leads to his need for constant stimulation. Your son's refusal to work may, in fact, be triggering you to mimic your own father's anger. You may even find yourself remembering a time when your father contained his anger by pouring himself into his work. Nothing — not even emotion — exists in isolation.

As science increases our capacity to penetrate the workings of matter, the interconnected web that sustains the world becomes more and more apparent. The Buddha was bold enough to state that there is no substantial reality other than the web of relationship by which the world is knit together. Therefore, he concluded, the best way to help oneself is to serve the world and help relieve the suffering present in it.

Physicists have revealed a level of reality in which events are instantaneously transmitted across the universe. Our capacity to communicate across boundaries once considered inviolable — via the scanning electron microscope to the Internet — is remaking our understanding of our place in the universe. The cell phone and the Internet have given humanity access to its intrinsic connectivity in an explicit way. We face the difficulty of critiquing systems in which we are deeply embedded — some of which rely on our unknowing for their continued existence. Our challenge is to contemplate the whole spectrum of reality. Secrecy, mistrust, denial, and the withholding or obscuring of the truth create suffering and impede our capacity to respond appropriately — a lesson made patently clear in the case of the USS Juneau. We are being called upon to learn how to behave in new ways. And our best ally is open and honest communication.

In a competitive culture the idea of an open and honest exchange of information is a startling one, but we cannot afford to ignore it. Crisis fixes our attention on dysfunction and, at the same time, invites us to generate insight at a higher level. We need to explore the causes of our current dilemmas, accept and integrate responsibility in our actions, and move ahead. Our willingness to expose the secret that parts of the system are not working is our best hope of crafting one that does.

As long as we hold a complex of trauma we will perpetuate and project the issue onto the world at large. (How many times have you held an attitude toward something which, in the end, turns out to be your own projection and not the reality of the situation at all? I've done it more times than I care to list.) The current debate over global warming is a case in point. The last few years have been the warmest on record in modern times. Indicators of climate change are obvious to the entire world, and yet the debate continues, influenced by the points of view of people who are invested in maintaining the status quo. Like the scientists with the platypus and the navy with the survivors of the *USS Juneau*, even if we look at the evidence, we don't always see it for what it is.

A deep contemplation of our global situation will help remove the blinders and may offer some timely gifts. The result of deep contemplation is often some form of fusion where the object perceived, the perception, and the perceiver are one. Or, as a sutra from Indian philosophy puts it: "The mind becomes that which it dwells upon." Consciousness merges with the field of attention, and information about the deep structure of the field is extracted — perhaps so quickly that the observer doesn't consciously notice what is happening. New discoveries, solutions, or the illumination of problems may occur as a result of the attainment of fusion.

I suspect that some kind of intelligence is at work, pushing us to a reformation of understanding about who we are as humans and where we fit in the web of life. As traditional strategies of relating to the world undergo radical transformation, our challenge is to see our intrinsic connectedness to all life with a clear and unvarnished awareness. When we allow ourselves to accept the full range of information about ourselves and our world, and not just partial truths, energy that has been tied up in denial, resistance, and obstruction becomes available for emotional healing and the reframing of beliefs and practices. Our willingness to take off our blinders, discard the veils of secrecy, and remain open to hearing disagreeable information can lead us. And the fullness of our knowing will help us find appropriate ways to respond.

Additional Resources

INTERNET LINKS

http://www.dharma.org/insight/budpsych.htm
   This site has a good overview of basic Buddhist concepts. The site is sponsored by the Insight Meditation Society and The Barre Center for Buddhist Studies.

http://goertzel.org/dynapsyc/1998/QuantumDreams.html
   "On the quantum Psychodynamics of Dreams," Mark Germine. An essay with an interesting discussion of co-dependent arising and quantum field fluctuation.

BOOKS

Abrahamson, Dean E., editor; and Timothy Wirth, designer. *The Challenge of Global Warming*. Island Press, 1989. ISBN 0933280866

Eco, Umberto, author; and Alastair McEwen, translator. *Kant and the Platypus: Essays on Language and Cognition*. Harcourt Brace, 1999. ISBN 0151004471

Gribbin, John. *Hothouse Earth: The Greenhouse Effect and GAIA*. Grove Weidenfeld, 1991. Out of print.

Kurzman, Dan. *Left to Die: The Tragedy of the USS Juneau*. Pocket Books, 1995. ISBN 0671748742

HARRIET TUBMAN

Harriet Tubman was an African-American woman
who was raised a slave. She found the inner strength to
break free from oppression and headed North to freedom.
What she did next sets her apart from so many of the other brave
souls who made the journey from the South: she returned, again
and again, to guide others. Southern slave owners pooled their
funds and generated a large reward for her capture, but her
bravery, common sense, humor, and improvising mind
helped her outwit them. Tubman became a force for freedom
that inspired people to call her the Moses of her time.

They say Miss Tubman held a pistol in her hand and quelled a mutiny. I'm here to say that she did. I know 'cause I was there. I know 'cause it was me who wanted to turn back. Can you even begin to understand what it means to be running North to freedom? Oh, I wanted it, believe me, I did. But when it came time to claim it, the fear ran deep.

I was shaking the day she pulled out the gun and aimed it at me, saying, "I got no time for this nonsense. You will be free." She had seen my urge to bolt before I even understood it had become a reality within my heart. That was the kind of leader she was. She knew her passengers better than we knew ourselves.

She was smart. I don't mean book-learning smart. I mean the kind of smart that reads the world and knows exactly what to do. She understood what made men do what they do, and she knew how to make them see what they wanted to see. Like the time she was in the South and saw her old master while she was helping some of us escape. She had chickens in her hand. She let them go and chased after them, moving herself out of harm's way. Who'd bother a slave chasing chickens? She was crafty; Miss Tubman was truly crafty.

Another time she took a train south when they were closing in on her. It never occurred to them that she would be coming back into the very trap they had so elegantly set. She was like that, turning things around all the time.

She sure turned me around. Made a brave man out of me even if it took the business end of a pistol to convince me. Though I must confess it was not the pistol that changed my heart. No, not at all. It was the glare in her eyes that did me in. She could look mean! There was no nonsense about her, except when she was cracking a joke. And she told plenty of them.

I found out about her headaches after I got to know her. And when I watched her black out one time I knew it was no joke at all. Her master had hit her with a weight for trying to interfere with the punishment of another slave. Damaged her for life he thought, but what he did was make a leader out of her. That's what he did.

Some people take their pain and grow weak. She took her pain and grew strong. She grew as strong as the fine old oak I played in as a child — the tree I used to hide in to get away from the misery of my world. She took her master's violence and forged a strength that helped free my people.

She took hundreds of us slaves North. Hundreds of scared people like myself, and she never lost one of us. She came back nineteen times to the South — some say twenty. I don't really care who's right. I just know she came back again and again. A $40,000 bounty on her head, and she came back to help free her people.

I didn't know what courage was until I met Harriet Tubman. And I'm telling you I studied her something fierce, 'cause I wanted to know the source of that courage. I asked her once and she said, "It ain't me. It couldn't be. I've got a guardian angel, that's what I have. They come when you think of others more'n yourself. They come like bees to honey."

Some call her a Moses to her people. Not having met Moses, I can't really say. What I do know is that she had courage enough to stand down my fear and the fear of my people — a fear that had gathered like a storm of darkness around our hearts. I know how hard it was for me to decide to go North, and I can't even think of returning South without getting a queasy feeling. She had the courage to make the journey to freedom and then turn around, again and again, to help save her people.

You should've seen her in the woods. She knew how to live in the woods like the sun spells the time of the day. She was a ghost in the trees when she needed to be, and like a magician she could make us ghosts too. She knew which roots to eat, which bark to take, and how to snare small animals for food. More than anything else, she knew which direction to go.

I don't know if you've ever been in the forest, but if you have, you'll know that directions can get mighty twisted in the darkness there. It's hard to know what's north or what's south. Miss Tubman, she would stand still next to some old grandmother of a tree and it would just come to her, which way she should go. If you ever need to find your way in a difficult world, you won't go wrong if you think on my dear friend, Miss Harriet Tubman.

Chapter *Four*

A BLUE BEAR, ECONOMICS, AND THE PACE OF OUR MODERN WORLD

I WAS DRIVING OUT TO A RETREAT north of Juneau late one night. As I came around a curve I saw a group of cars pulled off to the side of the road and some teenagers standing around something lying on the pavement. It looked like a human body. As I got closer, I realized that the form wasn't human; it was a smallish bear.

I pulled over and walked back toward the group. In a strange state of fearlessness, I moved closer to the bear, determined to aid him if I could. (A foolish thought in retrospect.) As I approached I saw him die.

I knelt down and placed my hand upon his still, warm head. He was a glacier bear, with a bluish and extraordinarily beautiful coat that is the result of a rare genetic anomaly, in which normally black fur is traded for a color not unlike the blue of the glaciers. He was lying on his belly, arms outstretched above his head, back legs curled against his body like a small sleeping baby. The teenagers all fell silent, and together we sat with the bear's death, with loss, and became midwives to the passing of the bear into another realm.

The bear's death was a potent depiction of the collision between the pace and concerns of our human world and that of the natural world. The collision has consequences for us, too. Consider the following scenario. Due to malfunctioning computers, shipping manifests are confused, and executives of a major corporation are out looking for their product containers on the waterfront of a major port. Air traffic control goes down at a capital city airport. The 911 emergency system fails in a city of many millions. ATM machines refuse to function properly. The reservations systems of the two biggest airlines go off-line at the same time. Major Internet providers are rendered nonfunctional. Credit card transactions are halted, and a local telephone company compromises millions of users when a switching computer goes down. A major American city is subject to a blackout, forcing planes to divert and businesses to close, and trapping people inside elevators. The lowered earnings report of a single large U.S. company sends the stock market down over three hundred points in one day. And the National Security Agency (NSA), the United States' top secret intelligence-gathering agency, goes down for four days as a consequence of computer error.

Is this science fiction fantasy? An apocalyptic snapshot of our world dreamt up in some novelist's mind? On the contrary, these events have all taken place, most of them during the last six months of 1998. And every systems failure — from the failure of the air traffic control system in the Salt Lake City Airport to the 911 system failure in Los Angeles — had real-world consequences, some of which were life threatening.

The extent to which we rely on the systems and infrastructures that support our activities also makes us vulnerable to them. In the fall of 1998, the near collapse of an obscure hedge fund (Long Term Capital Management) threatened to destabilize the entire world economic system. If the hedge fund had collapsed, $1.25 trillion in derivative-based bets would have shaken the global financial community to its foundations.

Derivatives are representative of a whole class of money-management tools that depend on the capacity of modern computers to transfer information at speed. Using data from numerous fluctuating pools of information — from weather conditions to financial market behavior — derivatives are so extremely complex that a Nobel Prize in Mathematics was given to one of their chief architects.

In effect, the near meltdown of the world economy was brokered by a handful of people working from sophisticated computer stations. They were able to leverage $2.2 billion in capital from investors into a $1.25 trillion house of cards. An unexpected shift in the movement of money — due to a default by Russia — was not anticipated by the complex computer programs that choreographed the hedge fund's activities. The rate of collapse was dramatic: within just a few days, the unstable hedge fund was threatening the entire world. In the end a consortium of fourteen of the world's largest financial institutions came to the rescue with a $3.6 billion bailout.

With computer trading and an interconnected financial system, money-making that maximizes profits while ignoring social and environmental needs can easily be amplified across the globe. While checks and balances to slow runaway trading exist in the world's exchanges, an inherent instability remains. In part, the recent meltdown of the Asian economies was due to a rerouting of capital by foreign investors that suddenly left countries like Indonesia without support. Ecological devastation followed hard on the heels of economic hardship as the poor scoured forests for fuel and for exotic animals to kill or capture for sale on the world market. Investors whose main criterion for investing is profit — not the health of the communities in which they invest — have little reason to pay attention to feedback from people negatively affected by those investments.

Our current economy is a religion. Sensitivity to suffering is lost in the din of a marketplace that has become the organizing principle for millions of people and a focus of energy around the world. It has become the new temple, a ceremonial gathering place with its own language and code of ethics. And it is a temple that is fundamentally too small to house the true gifts of humanity.

Whereas in past civilizations temples and places of worship were afforded the best technology and the most investment, we now have mercantile palaces erected across the planet. Commerce has become a ubiquitous presence in the hearts and minds of many of the most creative and industrious people in the world, displacing a worldview in which contact with a more substantial realm of being was held as not only possible but also attainable.

In the only recorded act of violence performed by Christ two thousand years ago, he threw the moneychangers out of the temple. Note that Christ did not chase the moneychangers from the community; he merely threw them out of the ground where contact with the eternal can be made. We need to restore a priority of spiritual attention to our concerns and activities in the world.

The pace of financial transactions needs to be moderated by more humanitarian and environmental considerations. A return to parity between work done and money earned would help slow the pace. When earnings are pegged to the actual time it takes to perform real work rather than being inflated by speculation, a respect for the pace of natural systems is reintroduced.

A shift in behavior away from acquiring goods and services and toward harvesting is called for. In a traditional harvest, the bounty of the Earth is gathered as a gift from the turning of the seasons. Lean times are respected and winter is seen as a time of rest. A true harvest pauses for the beauty of the moment, remembers the limits of the bioregion, and is based on gratitude not greed.

Personal tithing of time, energy, and money back to the common good is a real and necessary antidote to the large-scale injustices brought about by disparities of wealth. Opening one's heart to the suffering of the world and finding an authentic response is another way to equalize artificial concentrations of power.

To assume that the global economy will continue to support unsustainable practices is to place one's well-being in the hands of forces that have already caused the impoverishment of 40 percent of the world's population. Begin investing in local businesses. Support creative, life-affirming enterprises in your own community. Reward caring and considerate people with your own dollars.

Money should reflect real work done; then worth is derived from the work you are capable of doing, not the wealth you own. If this basic principle were followed much of the damage created by speculation would be mitigated. The self-confidence that comes from knowing your own worth gives meaning to life and can help keep you stable in the face of rapidly shifting outer circumstances. With meaning comes faith, and with faith comes the hope that we can create a better world.

To those who would scoff and say that such attitudes are out of touch with the realities of the modern world I would say: examine the stories of Gandhi and Mother Teresa. Both individuals were able to effect world change based on their personal compassion for human suffering. They were not rich, well connected, politically powerful, nor well known when they began to live their compassion. One freed a nation without using violence; the other transformed the care of the utterly poor and challenged attitudes about poverty worldwide.

Long ago the Buddha observed the human condition and pondered how greater peace of mind might be achieved. He noted that right livelihood was one of the essential foundations of inner peace. He counseled those who would follow his teachings to seek out work which did not cause suffering. He understood what any good ecologist also realizes: energy exchanged within natural systems must be kept balanced. Too much taken and not enough put back will devastate a forest, kill off an ocean, and make for suffering everywhere.

The issue has gone far beyond old solutions and old ways of operating. We are invited to be wide open to new possibilities, new avenues of communication, new solutions. We must continue to stretch our own personal limits and even be willing to surrender cherished beliefs. This means we each need to examine all aspects of our lives — from how we interact with our loved ones or spend our money to how we pray in the sanctuaries of our most private moments. I believe we are in the midst of a paradigm shift. I cannot pretend to know what the new paradigm will look like, but I can feel its presence pressing like water against the hull of a ship.

As we consider useful solutions, it is worth hearing the stories of two Latin American social experimenters. Gustavo Salas is a lean, wiry man. Looking into his eyes, you see the steadiness of someone who has tilled the soil of his life with great integrity. Born to a family of well-to-do Venezuelans, Gustavo and his three brothers all attended Yale. One brother recently ran for and lost the presidential race in Venezuela; the other two have become very successful businessmen. Gustavo took a different path. He moved into the barrios (the poorest section in cities) and adopted a life of voluntary simplicity.

With some friends Gustavo began a weekly meeting with those who lived in the barrio, during which people considered the problems before them and listened for a sense of intuitive guidance on how to solve them. Decisions were reached by consensus and then acted upon. The first problem the group tackled was transportation.

Adequate transportation was lacking in the barrio — a limiting factor in the lives of the poor. Working from the ground up, Gustavo and his friends managed to create a viable transportation system. So viable that the government felt threatened and briefly jailed him and other community leaders, accusing them of running a revolutionary movement. Which indeed they were, but it was a revolution of the human spirit.

After getting out of jail Gustavo and his friends looked at the few buses they had left and thought they could put vegetables in the seats and start a food distribution system. Their successful system is outperforming all capital-driven models in the area. The group is able to deliver food at lower cost to the very poor and still maintain a better economic output.

This self-organizing cooperative is a wonderful model of human ingenuity, compassion, and the power that comes from trusting intuitive guidance. Each member of the co-op makes the same amount of money. Gustavo and his wife live on $4,000 each annually, as do the rest of the members of the co-operative. Leadership tasks are rotated, and personal issues are worked out in the small-circle model. The kicker of the story is that it is such an economic success. Here is a clear and compelling example of how economies might be restructured to serve the communities in which they are embedded.

Another blossoming of hope took place in Columbia, just a short journey from Gustavo's barrio.[1] In 1971, Paolo Lugari saw the face of the future staring at him in the inhospitable llanos. Politically Colombia was in shambles, and it was clear that deforestation and population growth were marginalizing people. One of the more desolate landscapes on the planet, the llanos was an unlikely location to create a self-sustaining and ecologically mindful community. However, Paolo convinced Jorge Zapp, head of mechanical engineering at Bogota's Universidad de los Andes, to join him. Jorge brought a collection of graduate students and other inventive folk, and they began creating technology that was Earth-friendly and, ultimately, people-friendly.

Their inventions include: a non-polluting tannery; a cheap blend of local soil and cement that can be used for paving roads and runways; gaskets made of palm leaves; palm-oil-based feed supplements; solar collectors and biogas generators; micro-hydro turbines; and innovative pumps — such as a hydraulic ram that uses river flow to move a piston that pumps water. And, after 58 attempts, a windmill that is sufficiently adapted to local conditions that it will harness the slightest breeze and last for years without repair.

People began to gather around this center of invention, and a community was born. The people of Gaviotas elected not to patent their inventions but turned the creativity of their collective will to the good of the whole, and the town began to find its economic feet.

It was not always easy. Guerrillas, drug wars, and envious rivals all tried to bring "reality" to the dream on the llanos. But Gaviotas succeeded in holding to its collective vision of a community empowered by creative action, mutual support, and respect for the Earth. They managed to create a viable economy that is not based on speed and maximum consumption. The success of their community tells us that there are workable alternatives to the dominant economic paradigm.

In surveying the terrain of money and society it is worth considering for a moment the greatest wealth transfer in the history of the cosmos: the moment the universe sprang into being. Several aspects of that event are worth pondering. First, the Big Bang was not necessarily one distinct point that erupted; instead it appears to have been a leaping into being of a whole interconnected continuum, which may very well define our ability to understand its spatial shape. Space and time were still in the process of becoming what we know today. Another significant feature of the birth of the universe was the 300-thousand-year-long womb that ensued after the initial impulse arose. For approximately 300 thousand years the universe was so hot that its plasma field did not allow light to radiate. Then as the plasma cooled the universe suddenly went transparent. Light began to radiate beyond what had been the thermal boundary of this initial womb. Light has been radiating ever since, and the business of star making and planet forming got underway in earnest.

Allow me the poetic license to draw two analogies from this early transfer of wealth. First, the initial gesture of the universe to give arose as an interconnected impulse with no definite point of origin: it was simply a spontaneous eruption across a developing field of creation. That means that there is a model in the universe of wealth being spontaneously released across an interconnected field — a point worth considering in relation to money and an emerging ethic of wealth transfer and economic redistribution. In practical terms this means opening the flux of money to a more spontaneous and generous field of intention.

Interestingly, a mathematical model of economies created by two scientists — Jean-Philippe Bouchard and Marc Mézard — shows that without the system becoming "hot" by the movement of money at higher rates and to more diverse sources, the laws of physics and mathematics point to the inevitability of the rich staying super rich at the expense of others. In other words the only way to equalize economies is to make sure that they radiate.[2] One might be skeptical of such scientific excursions into finance except that Bouchard created a risk management company that has won the respect of the finance industry. He has proven that his theories work in the real world.

The second analogy has to do with the importance of gestation and of transparency in relation to the transfer of wealth. The moment the universe went transparent is, to me, one of the most astonishing images in all of nature. Consider the miracle of that moment when light suddenly begins to radiate after 300 thousand years of gestation in the most intense heat imaginable. Who knows what mysterious intermingling, what self-organizing systems arose, what quantum entanglements took place in that 300 thousand years-long? (It has been proven both theoretically and experimentally that once particles entangle at a quantum level, they stay connected and can communicate instantaneously across space and time.)

The analogy in the world of economics might run something like this: heat is a function of activity. And wealth is most often accrued through some form of intense activity. If the individual containers of our lives should become transparent too soon, then the internal coherence necessary to help seed a self-organizing system could be violated. Likewise if the containers were not allowed to become transparent and radiate, then further creative processes would be impossible, and the stars of our dreams would fail to materialize.

If you listen to the stories of successful entrepreneurs they will often talk about a critical point in their businesses where they became wildly successful: some kind of turning point in their growth process was attained and they suddenly "went transparent," making their goods and services more available for distribution. It may well be that our economies would be best served if we were to follow the path of radiance taken by the universe at the beginning of time.

In the next decade or so it is estimated that somewhere near $11 trillion will change hands as one generation gives way to the next. And it is estimated that the wealthiest families in North America could give $250 billion a year without eroding their basic way of life. I would like to make a case that financial generosity coming from the heart can make an enormously worthwhile contribution to the economic equation. And I would also make a case that the proper use of such generosity can help tip us into a more equitable economic system. How? By mimicking natural ecosystems, cosmic ecology, and some very old indigenous social practices.

Nature spends itself abundantly in order to sustain diversity and to ensure the continuation of future generations. The salmon runs in the part of Alaska where I live used to be so great that the streams were literally choked with fish at the end of every summer. At the same time, berry production in the muskeg, meadows, and hillsides would explode as the land gave of itself in a biological burst of abundance.

Move beyond the planet, and we see a similar pattern. Every once in a while, the internal mechanism that maintains the equilibrium of stars becomes unstable. The enormous pressures of nuclear fusion outstrip the star's capacity to radiate energy at a measured rate, and the star becomes a supernova, expending its energy in one enormous radiance. The disturbance caused by supernovas pushes against nearby intersteller gases and ultimately results in the formation of new stars.

If nature can give away its bounty with such abundance, then why can't the human community? Historically, some communities did. First Nations people in the Pacific Northwest organized regular potlatches in which individuals gained social and spiritual benefits by giving away much of their tangible wealth — an exercise in economic redistribution that may have helped stabilize their culture over hundreds of generations.

It is the habit of the universe to give. Maintaining tight control over money, protecting one's assets, and living from a Darwinian perspective of survival of the fittest may create sinkholes in the ecology of economics that will doom the system in the long run. When the capacity to give becomes an anchor point of one's identity and stature, the synthesis of spirituality with rightful economic activities can help restore integrity to a system that is currently failing to meet the needs of the planet. In the end, as in the beginning, this is about love.

Notes

1. See Alan Weisman, *Gaviotas: A Village to Reinvent the World* (Chelsea Green, 1999).
   See also http://dharma-haven.org/five-havens/weisman.htm for the transcript of a documentary on Gaviotas.
   See also http://www.ilovethisplace.com/eco/livingtoday/gaviotas.html for an article on Gaviotas by Donnella Meadows.
2. See Mark Buchanan, "That's the Way the Money Goes," *New Scientist*, August 2000.
   http://www.newscientist.com/features/features.jsp?id=ns225217

Additional Resources

INTERNET LINKS

http://www.ifg.org/ International Forum on Globalization

http://www.tompaine.com/news/2000/01/04/6.html
   TomPaine.com Article: "Out-of-Control CEO Salaries: Should Taxpayers Subsidize Them?" by Morton Mintz.

http://www.indg.org/global.htm
   International Network on Disarmament and Globalization.

http://www.wilpf.int.ch/~wilp/globalizationtoc.htm
   Woman's International League for Peace and Freedom web page on Globalization.

http://www.aflcio.org/paywatch/index.htm
Executive PayWatch: The AFL-CIOs web site for monitoring corporate pay.

BOOKS

Collins, Chuck, Betsy Leondar-Wright, and Holly Sklar. *Shifting Fortunes: The Perils of the Growing American Wealth Gap.* United for a Fair Economy, 1999. ISBN 0965924920

Douthwaite, Richard. *Growth Illusion.* New Society Publishers, 1999. See especially the Epilogue. ISBN 0865713960

Henderson, Hazel. *Beyond Globalization: Shaping a Sustainable Global Economy.* Kumarian Press, 1999. ISBN 1565491076

Karliner, Joshua. *The Corporate Planet: Ecology and Politics in the Age of Globalization.* Sierra Club Books, 1997. ISBN 0871564343

Korten, David C. *The Post-Corporate World: Life After Capitalism.* Berrett-Koehler, 1999. ISBN 1576750515

—————. *When Corporations Rule the World.* Berrett-Koehler, 1996. ISBN 1887208011

Lapham, Lewis H. *The Agony of Mammon: The Imperial Global Economy Explains Itself to the Membership in Davos, Switzerland.* Verso Books, 1998. ISBN 1859847102

Mander, Jerry. *In the Absence of the Sacred: The Failure of Technology and the Survival of the Indian Nations.* Sierra Club Books, 1992. ISBN 0871565099

Mander, Jerry, and Edward Goldsmith, eds. *The Case Against the Global Economy And For a Turn Toward the Local.* Sierra Club Books, 1997. ISBN 0871568659

Martin, Hans-Peter and Harald Schumann, authors; and Patrick Camiller, translator. *The Global Trap: Globalization and the Assault on Prosperity and Democracy.* Zed Books, 1997. ISBN 1856495302

Schaeffer, Robert K., ed. *Understanding Globalization: The Social Consequences of Political, Economic, and Environmental Change.* Rowman & Littlefield, 1997. ISBN 0847683524

Weisman, Alan. *Gaviotas: A Village to Reinvent the World.* Chelsea Green, 1998. ISBN 0930031954

Dmitri Mendeleyev

Dmitri Mendeleyev was a scientist whose gift to the
world was the periodic table of elements. His capacity to see order
where before it had been hidden was the inner gift of his life.
Mendeleyev became a national treasure in Russia,
and the whole country mourned when he died.
In this vignette, I have taken the liberty of speaking
directly from his point of view.

It was the glass blower, Timofei, who first introduced me to my work. He was a meticulous man who had the heart of an artist. I would watch him in front of the kilns, the flames red upon his face, and be mesmerized by the beauty he brought into this world.

I remember one day watching him as he gave his breath to a spinning, glowing, orb of glass. As the glass slowly congealed and took on the hardness of its permanent shape, he smiled at me and said, "Dmitri, do not forget that everything is Art!"

Timofei had order in his soul, an order that he breathed into his art. His tools were simple but well cared for, and when he reached for them they were always there.

He taught me that early, saying, "Dmitri, polish your tools with your attention."

He would laugh at me now, no doubt, with my beard and hair so long — long enough to challenge the birds to build a nest in the tree of myself. He would probably chide me for not tending to my appearance. But I would tell him, "Timofei, I am still polishing the tools that are truly important to me — the ideas which live within my mind. It is the polish on them which lets me draw closer to the truth.

Those ideas! Bessargin, my aunt's husband, gave me the first ideas. He had come to join us in Siberia because his politics had gotten too hot. He used to joke with me, saying, "Dmitri, it takes a land as cold as your Siberia to keep my blood from boiling."

I remember my walks with him on those cold winter mornings when frost crystals caught the first light of the day. He would say, "Dmitri, what do you see?"

"I see beauty."

"Keep looking, Dmitri. What do you see?

"I see light coming from the ground."

"Keep looking, Dmitri. What do you see?"

"I see light reflecting from the faces of the crystals."

"Good, Dmitri. That is a start. When you finally know

what you see, you will be a scientist. And remember, everything is Science."

If it had not been for my mother, Maria, Timofei and
Bessargin would have had not such a great effect on me. She
worked hard after my father died to support all my brothers
and sisters. She worked hard, but she never let her work hold
her spirit hostage.

Even after the fire at the glass works where she was
manager, she kept believing in life. And in me. When we had
to leave Siberia, the land of such beauty and such warm people,
even then her spirit was untarnished. What was her secret?
It was simple. "Everything is Love." She was like one of the
frost crystals that held the secret of light.

I loved those crystals. There was something deep in their
structure that spoke to me, urged me, prodded me to find the
map of the hidden realms of matter. Oh yes I, Dmitri
Mendeleyev, have always searched for the secret of everything.

And I found order. Oh yes, when it became apparent to
me that there was a pattern to the elements, a periodicity,
it was like I was looking at the reflection of light through
a crystal from one of my childhood mornings. My mother,
Bessargin the rebel scientist, Timofei the glass blower,
and the cold clear air of Siberia — these were the teachers
who helped me.

And so I urge you — look for yourself for the ways that crystals can reflect light. Look to find the order behind appearances, look until you know something about the maker of this universe and how he brings order to this world. The world will tell you its secrets. Just look.

Chapter Five

RESTORING TIME

A S WINTER SOLSTICE ARRIVES once again and the planet comes to a still point of rest in its cosmic wobble, a Hopi elder sits atop a mesa watching the canopy of stars that maps the skies of her homeland. Hours will pass as she considers the prophecies of her people. Memories of her people's migrations through many worlds wrap around her like a shawl. She is part of a much larger story of creation — her place in time anchored by the unfolding of her tribe's wisdom.

For a Yu'pik hunter alone on the ice, solstice arrives in a stillness only the Arctic can hold. Space unfolds in the vault of the sky and along the nearly flat horizon. Time — the mistress of space — correspondingly stills, then moves again. Now light can begin to edge back into the darkness that has wrapped the hunter's homeland; no more meaningful time can be found in the seasons of his experience.

The flow of the river and the cycle of the sun are the chronometers of a modern Egyptian woman's experience: cycles of return that have been witnessed for thousands of years by generations of the woman's ancestors. On the ceiling of a nearby temple is an image of Nut, the sky goddess who swallows the sun and gives birth again to light. Stars ripple through the wavy lines of cosmic energy that make up Nut's form. In the ancient hieroglyphics that encoded the image painters' understanding, there is no word for past or present, only symbols that describe an immanent being-ness out of which all events unfold. The woman walks to the river, savoring the morning birdsong and drawing in the nourishment necessary for the coming day. She is simply at home on the river-banks of her people.

For the manager of an automobile assembly line in Flint, Michigan, the solstice will come and go unmarked. Orders will be filled, glitches fixed, and personality issues resolved. The movement of the planet will pass unnoticed by a man whose life is anchored in a compression of time that is the twenty-four-hours-a-day, seven-days-a-week production schedule of the plant.

We can say a few things about time, and we can certainly examine the impact of how humans relate to time in their world. Time is a consequence of our unfolding universe. Time is relative. Time is influenced by motion. Cyclic processes measure time. Time is rhythm.

If we are to understand the challenges of our era, we must understand our relationship to time, for much of the difficulty we face in our modern world is predicated on how we conceptualize its motion. Biology determines some of our experience of time.[1] Intricate metabolic pathways in our bodies — synchronized to the movement of the sun and Earth — loop in cycles and act like clocks that are set by the phasing of light and dark. These internal molecular clocks determine our perception of time and account for our feeling that time sometimes moves at different rates.

Alterations in body chemistry also alter our subjective experience of time. Remember what time was like when you were a child? When we are young our body metabolism is set at a faster rate; consequently, time seems more spacious. A day for a child can seem an eternity, whereas for an adult a day can seem to speed by in a moment. In adults the biological process of falling in love releases hormones and other chemicals that alter our internal processing of time. A moment with the one you love becomes an eternity, and a moment away from them is also associated with an eternity. Diet affects body chemistry, as do hormone-mimicking chemical compounds in the environment. Drugs and alcohol are two other powerful modifiers of body chemistry that seem to alter time.

Our experience of time is profoundly conditioned by culture, as anyone who has waited for a bus in India, tried to catch a plane in Egypt, or gone out to shop in Italy in the afternoon has discovered.

On a somewhat larger scale, the observation of natural rhythms conditions our experience of time. The fact that we are born, live, and die creates in us a sense of time and its movement that affects our fears, hopes, and aspirations. Movements of the sun across the sky (a function of the Earth's rotation), the lunar cycle (from full moon to full moon), and the seasons (the result of the majestic motion of the poles as they lean toward the sun and away again) are an obvious triad that mark the passage of time. While we are able to chronicle its passing, the actuality of what time is continues to be something of a mystery — if you reach out to touch it you are apt to find it elusive. Like gravity, which is difficult to experience directly, time is most often experienced through its effects.

Is there an objective time that remains the same outside our perceived subjective experience? Not really. Step off the globe and we find that time and space are both conditioned by gravity. Suns, planets, and moons all warp the fabric of time and space, shifting the flow of these fields in ways that are difficult to visualize. Factor in the complexity of an expanding universe, with objects receding from one another at enormous speeds, and suddenly time is stretched, modified, molded, and shaped to a surprising degree.

As an adolescent, Einstein performed a thought experiment in which he imagined that he was going as fast as the speed of light. Most adolescents enjoy challenging authority, but this particular teenager was about to unseat the accepted worldview of his age: he saw that time and space are related — an idea that was to gestate and emerge a decade later as his special theory of relativity. Einstein was to show that time responds to fluctuations of space and, inversely, space responds to the movement of time. In the now famous example of someone traveling at a rate approaching the speed of light, he pointed out that time would slow down relative to an observer on Earth. Time is influenced by motion. And the perception of time is relative to the position of the observer. There is no metronome in heaven beating out the same time everywhere in the universe. Time is relative.

Western culture is predicated on just the opposite notion: that time is absolute. We organize our lives around clocks, schedules, and deadlines that divide time into fixed increments. (Try and find a word for "deadline" in any indigenous culture and I believe you will come up short.) I would argue that our reliance on mechanistic time systems that are divorced from larger natural systems create schisms that erode our mental stability, quality of life, and ultimately our environment.

Mechanistic models — clock and watch ideas of time — are not the only way to conceptualize time. Numerous cultures throughout history have conceived of and experienced time as a spiral: the same structure that we now know encodes genetic information and organizes galaxies. Even our solar system traces a graceful spiral as each planet circles the sun, continuously entering a new place in space and time relative to the galactic center.

Return a culture to a sense of sacred time and you will find that you can live in a world that renews itself, that returns again and again to where it begins. You are released from the compelling need to accomplish everything tomorrow. (Interestingly, the most astute inner technologies of spiritual change on the planet were most often developed in cultures that based their lives on circular time.) If renewal is not part of a culture's worldview and time is a one-way arrow, then the burden of solving life's dilemmas becomes onerous. From the ancient Chinese in eastern Asia to the Maya of Meso-America, time was understood as something sacred, a meaningful flow intimately linked to the unfolding story of their people. Their relationship to the entire universe was seen as the unfolding of a creative purpose with the field of time. Observatories erected by earlier cultures, from Chaco Canyon or Stonehenge to the city plan of Teotihuacan in central Mexico, were remarkably accurate for gauging the movement of the heavenly bodies and predicting the passage of time. And in Meso-America activities ranging from courtship to the planting of foodstuffs were timed to occur in accordance with rhythms depicted in a cosmological grid. (The ancient calendar-makers of Meso-America even predicted the acceleration and potential breakdown of modern society.)

In Western thought, time became unhinged from circularity and became a one-directional arrow called progress — pointing toward the future. About 96 AD on the Island of Patmos off the coast of Asia Minor, a man banished for his revolutionary activities put ink to parchment and described a vision he had been shown. When the man finished his final line and put down his pen, the waves of the sea were still peacefully lapping at the rock of the island upon which he stood, as they would continue to do for nearly two thousand more years. But the waves St. John unleashed on Western concepts of time with his Book of Revelation were far more tumultuous.[2]

According to John's vision time is a finite process with a definite termination date. Events are expected to escalate as the forces of good and evil seek to do battle near an end time. Finally, after a titanic battle that is to lay waste to most of the world, Christ will appear in the second coming. All who are saved will be lifted from the carnal battlefield of polar opposites and into a new heaven and Earth.

Several attitudes about time are embedded in or follow from John's story: time and matter are prisons that the holy person longs to be freed from. Time is an onerous burden, calling for patience and forbearance. There is always a final judgment in which time is annihilated. The preoccupation with being saved at some future time gives one the right to abuse other human beings and destroy the Earth. It is always better to live for the end result than to pay too much attention to the means — in other words: progress at any price.

How much of St. John's apocalyptic vision was a result of unconscious programming from the literary devices of his time? The genre of apocalyptic writing had already been maturing for nearly two hundred years. Obscure numerological formulations, strong allegorical imagery, and the presence of a guiding angel all of which are found in the Book of Revelation are typical of this genre. How much was an attempt to wrestle some degree of personal power from a situation of powerlessness? Patmos is small — only five miles wide by eleven miles long — and must certainly have contributed to his sense of containment and imprisonment. How much was driven by the revolutionary status of the early church, fighting as it was for its very life against a large oligarchy? Revolutionaries tend to be driven by polarization into positions that are dogmatic and allow for little ambiguity or compromise. The Book of Revelation could easily be read as a book of revolution. Its strident tone, depiction of an ultimate battle between good and evil, and predictions of the end of time are characteristic rhetorical elements used by many radical groups trying to subvert the power of a dominant paradigm. Whatever the source of St. John's vision and writing — and there is considerable debate about who the man on Patmos was — the Book of Revelation illustrates linear attitudes about time and humanity's relationship to it that was to become a legacy of the Christian era.

St. John's abstractions about time did not stand alone in early Western thought, however. Calendars are based on another kind of abstraction of time, and the history of Western calendars illustrates our tendency to see time as an entity to be manipulated — regardless of what information the calendar makers used. The original Roman calendar was based on a mercantile model and was adjusted to a seven-day week after contact with Egypt. During the time of the Roman Empire various authorities arbitrarily adjusted the calendar to prolong their stay in elected positions, until Julius Caesar attempted to put an end to this practice by standardizing the calendar. His calendar — the Julian — may have been based on an integration of the solar, lunar, and steller maps of the pre-Roman cultures. The

Julian system was widely used by European countries until the Catholic Church, the leading power in the world at the time, decided to augment its own calendar.

Pope Gregory, drawing on the work of a seventh-century monk named Brother Bede, instituted the Gregorian calendar in the late 1500s. This calendar — the one most commonly used now — was based on ancient Babylonian observations as modified by the Egyptians and the philosophical underpinnings of the early Christians. The West's manipulation of calendars didn't end there, either.

If we jump ahead 150 years or so, the British, who were emerging as a world power, decided to join the Catholic Church and decreed in 1752 that they would abide by the Gregorian calendar. To harmonize the calendars they ordered that 1752 should end with December 31st rather than continue until the following March 25th (the traditional New Year of the Julian calendar) and that September 2, 1752, should be called September 14, 1752. So, at the convenience of British political will, nearly a quarter of 1752 was banished from the records. Each manipulation — from the Romans to the British — abstracted time for either gain or expediency and created schisms in our relationship with the natural world.

The clash between Western linear time and sacred circular time is epitomized in the four-hundred-year struggle between the First Nations people of this continent and European invaders — a struggle that continues right into modern times. The Vatican, as part of a consortium, wants to build an observatory in Arizona on a peak that is sacred to the Apache. Its purpose? The stated reason is that they want to be able to determine if there are any alien life forms in the universe so that they can send emissaries to convert them.

The land has been cleared and bulldozed for the observatory. On several occasions during the permit process the Vatican furthered their agenda by acting in a more timely manner than did the Apache. The Apache, who have essentially been a culture in hiding since the time of the internment camps, were reluctant to speak out. Furthermore, they were accustomed to deliberations calibrated by the movement of natural time. So now the same institution that imprisoned one of the founders of the scientific method — Galileo — has embroiled itself in a controversy over a mountain that carries some of the ancestral and sacred significance by which the Apache establish the meaning of their world.

We need to find ways to re-establish meaning in our relationship with time and with the ordered natural rhythm of rest and activity that is the signature of all natural systems. When the Dalai Lama's first meditation teachers began coming to the West, they took back many reports of the misery in Western psyches. The Dalai Lama couldn't believe that any class of humans could have so much internal misery, and he wanted to know why Westerners were so unhappy. A significant answer to his question can be found in how Westerners negotiate time.

If you break the hoop of time and create movement that has no renewal or return, there can be no rest. I believe that in the absence of sacred time many people use drugs and alcohol in an attempt to arrest that sense of precipitous speed so characteristic of Western life. With a return to a sense of sacred time you can access realms of consciousness from which our sense of meaning emerges — that deeper level of concentration and attention that enlivens and inspires us.

As a major portion of my life's work, I take people into the wilderness for spiritual retreats, and I have witnessed firsthand the tyranny of Western time and the enormous psychological damage it causes. I vividly remember one woman who was working overtime trying to put a business together that would succeed in the so-called real world. At the end of a short hike, during which the natural world was a constant source of irritation and annoyance to her, she slammed her pack down on the ground and stormed off. We set her tent up for her, and she withdrew into its relative security for several days. When she emerged, she was a different person. The tension that had been driving her was visibly absent, and there was an innocence and hopefulness in her face that hadn't been there before. I watched her really see the aspen trees around her for the first time.

The simple act of disconnecting from the tyranny of one-way time has enormous benefits. It takes most people about three days to step down into a more natural rhythm — one in which the cycles of the day, the moods of the heart, and the needs of the body are allowed to emerge and self-organize. When they do, I have seen people's dream life suddenly switch on. I have seen people arrive at solutions to seemingly insoluble problems simply by finally having the time to be. I have watched worry drain from faces and bodies begin to heal, all within the hoop of circular time offered by nature.

Most spiritual traditions have developed practices and techniques that enable individuals to deliberately alter their perception of time. We can look to some roots in the Western experience, and we can consider some lessons from other realms as well. We know Christ went into the desert for 40 days and 40 nights to fast and pray — a practice mirrored in other traditions. At Buddhist meditation retreats a bell will be rung at different times over the course of the day, whether during meals, talks, or meditation. When it rings you are invited to stop whatever you are doing and return to an awareness of your breath — a refreshing practice of mindfulness. Changing the blood respiration gases through the manipulation of the breathing process is another much-used technique that can return us to a sense of sacred time.

When the perception of time is altered using the body's own processes, there is nearly always an increase in environmental awareness. We slow down enough to notice the space between leaves, to become poetic, lyrical, and multidimensional in our comprehension of the world around us. If we limit the availability of this quality of time we engender a speediness of mind that can turn against and destroy its own world.

What can you do? Make more time in your life. This does not mean abdicating personal responsibility for managing time's demands, but it does mean inviting a temple of timelessness into our daily lives. A mind preoccupied with duties, deadlines, and future obligations has lost the ability to enter the sacredness of the present moment. Watching the sun rise and set, pausing at midday, and honoring the passing of the seasons can all help us realign with the deeply organic unfolding of time. Carve out a few days — or even a few hours — from your busy schedule. Find a quiet retreat or create one in your own home. Disconnect the phone, put away the computer, and learn to live within the rhythm of the day. Then pay attention to the messages that come bubbling up. These may seem like small, inconsequential acts in the face of escalating world issues, but like the Mississippi River that begins as a few rivulets in northern Minnesota, the collective force of many choosing to inhabit a mode of sacred time can and will have an effect. Take time to leave time behind. Ultimately, a healthy ecology of time is essential to the healthy ecology of the planet.

Notes

1. See http://sulcus.berkeley.edu/meb165/mcb165sp98tPaper/ mcb165sp98R.manuscript/-34.html "Going from External Cues to Behavioral Output: Understanding Biological Clocks" for an excellent paper on biological clocks.
   Also see www.srbr.org, the web site for the Society for Research on Biological Rhythms and http://cbt4pc.bio.virginia.edu, the website for the Center for Biological Timing.

2. See http://siscom.net/~direct/revelation/history%20overview.htm and http://www.ellenwhite.org/revdate.htm for information on the Book of Revelation.

Additional Resources

INTERNET LINKS

http://clavius.as.arizona.edu/vo/history.html
    The home page for the Vatican Observatory.

http://clavius.as.arizona.edu/vo/ecology.html
The Vatican Observatory's rebuttal to environmental critics.

http://clavius.as.arizona.edu/vo/indian.html
The Vatican Observatory's response to the Apache.

http://cougar.ucdavis.edu/nas/varese/122/Spring96/graham/nas_mt.g.html
Campo, John J. and Alexiss A. Holden. "Dzil Nchaa Si An: The San Carlos Apache vs. The Vatican." This is a well-written account of the Apache position on the Observatory.

http://planet-peace.org/archive/mt_graham/index.html
The Apache Survival Coalition's home page.

http://www.optdesig.com/Philosophy/Husserl.htm
An essay on Edmund Husserl's theories of time.

http://spiritshower.com/solar.htm
A description of how time is encoded in solar system events.

http://www.timesoft.com/hopi/index.html
The Hopi Way home page.

BOOKS

Ashby, Dr. Muata Abhaya. *The Cycles of Time*. Cruzian Mystic Books, 1997. ISBN 1884564135

Bender, John. "Introduction." In David Wellbery, ed. *Chronotypes: The Construction of Time*. Stanford University Press, 1991. ISBN 0804719128

Binkley, Sue. *The Clockwork Sparrow: Time, Clocks and Calendars in Biological Organisms*. Prentice Hall, 1990. Out of print. [Available at http://www.centurybooks.com/stacks/science.html]

Butterfield, Jeremy, ed. *The Arguments of Time*. Oxford University Press, 2000. ISBN 01972962074

Edinger, Edward F., author; and George R. Elder, editor. *Archetype of the Apocalypse: A Jungian Study of the Book of Revelation*. Open Court, 1999. ISBN 0812693957

Goldbeter, Alan. *Biological Oscillations and Cellular Rhythms: The Molecular Basis of Periodic and Chaotic Behavior*. Cambridge University Press, 1995.

Heidegger, Martin, author; and Theodore Kisiel, translator. *History of the Concept of Time: Prolegomena, Studies in Phenomenology and Existential Philosophy*. Indiana University Press, 1992. ISBN 025332730X

Le Poidevin, Robin, author; and Murray MacBeath, editor. *The Philosophy of Time*. Oxford University Press, 1993. ISBN 025332730X

Orlock, Carol. *Inner Time: The Science of Body Clocks and What Makes Us Tick*. Birch Lane Press, 1993. ISBN 1-559721944

The Journal of Biological Rhythms. SAGE Publications. ISBN 07487304

Thera, Nyanaponika and Bhikkhu Bodhi. *Abhidhamma Studies: Buddhist Explorations of Consciousness and Time.* Wisdom Publications, 1998. ISBN 0861711351

Winfree, Arthur T. *The Timing of Biological Clocks.* Scientific American Library, 1987. Out of print.

GANDHI AND THE SEA

Gandhi's simple lifestyle connected him with the rhythms of
Indian village life, which are modulated by the cycles of night
and day and by the seasons. His adherence to natural time
may have given him the strength to endure the political battles
he undertook for the liberation of his country.

He had wanted to be near the sea. Perhaps the ocean moving within him made him want to rest near the echo of a larger sea; when he walked its rhythms moved in his limbs. (I don't think it is possible to hold a nation in your heart and hide it from your body.) I had been with him long enough to know that he always paused before the really important campaigns — just as each wave of the sea comes to a point of rest before it crashes upon the shore. It was about salt this time. Just as it had been about weaving before. The salt tax imposed by the British allowed them to control a substance necessary to the life of every person in the country.

He had an instinct for what would move people. All through his travels across India, he had been harvesting. Like a fisherman who watches until the net is full, he waited for each moment to become full before he acted. That kind of patience has always struck me as the essence of wisdom. The British were masters of the seas, but he was about to claim the salt that ran like sand through their fingers. You think the English would have learned from their experience in America, but human memory is short, and human hearts grow cold so easily.

His heart was different. And it was that difference that made the revolution we accomplished all the more compelling. He had been beaten and jailed many times. He had been threatened, jeered at, laughed at, and feared by the British. If any man had a reason to hate his enemy, he did. But there was a flame in his heart that burned hot enough to consume his anger. He once told me, "I have learnt through bitter experience the one supreme lesson to conserve my anger, and as heat conserved is transmuted into energy, even so our anger controlled can be transmuted into a power which can move the world."

So you see, it was not that he did not feel anger. Some people laughed at his adherence to nonviolence, even questioned whether he had a human heart that felt the common emotions we all feel. He felt anger, but what he did with his anger, that is one of the great teachings of his life. He understood the alchemy of change. When he decided to accomplish something, he bent all of his energy to the task.

Even when he did not have the necessary skills he still stayed true to the task before him. Weaving was — well — not exactly his *forte*, but he wove with a dedication that was devotional.

I know he was unfailing in his self-examination. Whatever defect you might find in the world he was able to find somewhere within himself. His capacity to realize that the world within is a true mirror of the outer world gave birth to his compassion.

On one occasion he was to say, "There only is life where there is love. Life without love is death. Love is the reverse of the coin of which the obverse is truth. It is my firm faith that we can conquer the whole world by truth and love." Many could have crafted those words, but he took the fiery path of making them real. There by the sea, as he sat with the decision to oppose the salt tax, I saw both the heat of his anger and the fire of his love. Some say it was the turning point in our struggle for independence. All I know is that when he led the march to the sea to reclaim the salt from the waves, he walked with the will of someone who had made his anger a steel edge of uncompromising truth. And the darkness he dispelled in his lifetime shifted the foundations of our world.

Chapter Six

ALL THINGS RETURN IN TIME

THE DRIVE TO CHACO CANYON, New Mexico, is not particularly engaging. A long dirt road rambles among sagebrush and sandstone buttes, revealing an occasional building placed almost as an afterthought, as if someone had simply grown tired of the journey and decided to rest for a while. As the road curves down into a wash, a complex of dwellings and ritual circles known as kivas appears. Here, millions of hand-placed rocks have sculpted space into a coherent, concentrated focus.

On the top of a butte that rises from the wash, you'll find a series of markings on a slab of sandstone. The stone itself is shadowed by surrounding rock, but at winter solstice a dagger of light moves across its surface and aligns with the markings. The stone is an instrument for precisely tracking the motion of the Earth around the sun, and evidence that the inhabitants of the canyon were keenly aware of and interested in the recurring movements of celestial bodies. Their lives were linked to the cycles of a greater whole.

Episodic forces link the environment, the internal mechanisms of our bodies, even our feelings. And we are being called upon to re-awaken awareness and establish connection with these forces, which sweep through us in waves of energy. Some (such as light) are obvious; some (such as electromagnetic or gravitational forces) are invisible; and some are not yet known to science. But cycles exist everywhere.

The global ocean thermohaline circulation is one cycle that is known.[1] Involving the joint effects of temperature (thermodynamics) and salinity (haline dynamics), this cycle literally ties the oceans of our planet together and helps to modulate the weather. In one branch of this system, the Gulf Stream, warm, salty water near the surface of the Atlantic Ocean is carried northward to the vicinity of Iceland. During the winter months heat from this water is extracted by cold, westerly winds that flow across the Atlantic from North America. (The warmed air moderates winter conditions downwind in northern Europe.) The denser cooled water sinks to the abyss, forming the lower limb of the Atlantic's conveyor and transporting an average of 16 million cubic meters of water per second — comparable to the world's total rainfall, or 100 times the amount of water transported by the Amazon River.

Water carried by the Atlantic's lower limb passes around the southern tip of Africa, where it joins a powerful circum-Antarctic current. Fed by deep water generated beneath the ice shelves surrounding the Antarctic continent, the mixture flows northward into the deep Indian and Pacific Oceans where it eventually wells up to the surface. One of many ocean branches returns a flow westward, passing through the Indonesian Straits, across the Indian Ocean, and around the tip of Africa into the South Atlantic.

Even the massive movement of waters and energy transfer in the thermohaline cycle is in danger of disruption. The historical geologic record shows instances when the Gulf Stream has shut down abruptly over the course of only a few years. The phenomenon is thought to be caused by freshwater melting that dilutes the mixing zones in the North Atlantic where the ocean's conveyor belt turns back under itself and heads southward again. There is concern that with the acceleration of global warming and the rapid melting of glacial ice in the northern hemisphere this process may recur.

Move from the ocean to land and we find evidence of cycles in terrestrial events.[2] Earthquakes, precipitation, and floods are cyclic. Cycles of 9.6 to 9.7 years have been linked to fluctuations in coyote and salmon populations, storm track shifts in the North Atlantic, barometric pressures in France, and tree-ring widths in Arizona. Consider, too, the case of electricity in trees. An electrical current flows through trees, and it switches in regular cycles. For a period of time the current will flow up the tree, then reverse and flow down into the Earth. The switching effect occurs simultaneously throughout large forests, though the mechanism that induces a change in the direction of the current remains unclear.

Human activities exhibit cyclicality, too. A. L. Tchijevsky (a Russian professor), researching statistics and anecdotal evidence from 72 countries from 500 B.C. to 1922, found that there was a recurring cycle of unrest and excitability in world affairs every 11 years during this period — a cycle Tchijevsky posited was being driven by recurrent sunspot activity. Every nine years (nationwide in the U.S.) there is a peak in the number of people returning to some form of organized religion. Interestingly, the peak of this cycle coincides with the troughs of several nine-year business cycles that include: drops in bank deposits, cotton prices, and Canadian Pacific Railway ton-miles. When the business cycle peaks, attendance at churches hits a low point. (It makes sense from an intuitive point of view that when more people are tending to the exterior world, they have less time to monitor interior or religious functions.) Other episodic cycles occur in railroad stock prices, copper prices, steel production, auto sales, real estate transfers, and building construction.

Even our bodies exhibit cyclic behaviour. Molecular functioning appears to have a swirling vortex of timed cycles that pulse, vibrate, and support life. Ancient Chinese physicians observed that different organ systems had more, or less, chi (energy) in them at various times of the day. Modern studies in endocrinology have shown that hormones are released in very distinct time-modulated ways. All the glands — which support a host of bodily functions including our moods — appear to function according to systematically integrated rhythms. These physiological cycles are directly linked to the 24-hour light and dark cycle and to the shift of the seasons. Transformations in gene structure, oxidation cycles in a cell's energy system, fertility rates, and heartbeat are all linked through a cyclic interweaving with the movements of the Earth, the moon, and other celestial objects.

Edward R. Dewey — from whose data I have drawn for this discussion — was fascinated by cycles. After President Hoover asked him to investigate what had caused the Great Depression, Dewey spent the rest of his life searching for the causes behind the cycles he uncovered. (The foundation he began, The Foundation for the Study of Cycles, is still in existence.) By the end of a life-time of investigation, Dewey was convinced that forces originating beyond our planet are responsible for the incredible variety of synchronized cycles we observe here on Earth, though he did not claim to understand what those forces are.

Indeed, many planetary processes may be synchronized to larger universal processes (a view long held by astrologers from many cultures). In March 6, 1989, during the solar maximum of the sunspot cycle, a massive magnetic storm erupted on the surface of the sun, creating an x-ray flare that lasted for 137 minutes. A few days later, on March 8, a solar proton event began that matured into a major magnetic storm on March 13. The solar wind hit the magnetic field of the Earth, generating a power surge in telephone, electrical, and cable networks. In Canada more than a million people were left without power. By 1998, scientists had presented the first proof that sunspot cycles affect weather patterns — a powerful support for the idea that distant cycles can cause change in our local environment.

Sunspot cycles, in particular, command a great deal of interest. Like A. L. Tchijevsky and the scientists studying weather patterns, the ancient Mayans may have seen a connection between sunspot activity and occurrences here on Earth. The Mayan calendar — whose mathematical precision is now beyond scientific dispute — predicts a major shift of ages circa 2012. We know that the Earth's magnetic field has reversed at least once, and it has been postulated that a relationship exists between sunspot activity and magnetic field reversals. Maurice Cotterell[3] argues that the Mayan calendar encodes a precise knowledge of sunspot cycles, and according to one reading of Mayan prophecy, a field reversal could be the shift predicted for 2012.

Whether or not a field reversal is an actual possibility, the value of considering the Mayan perspective is that we can learn to see terrestrial events within the matrix of much larger forces. The mythologies, rituals, and customs used by ancient cultures to mediate between people and the powers of the natural world created a context of meaning by which they could make sense of change. We are being asked to undertake a similar process. An escalation of planetary events is conspiring to force us away from the secure life raft of rational understanding and into a multi-dimensional, intuition-based, right-brain comprehension of events — a reemergence of meaning, if you will. For modern Western sensibilities that give personal choice and freedom such a high value, the notion that large patterns of influence are affecting our world and behavior is anathema. The truth, however, is that we are conditioned by geophysical forces which are vastly beyond our control.

Processes of synchronization operate at levels beyond our conscious awareness and affect many aspects of our lives. If you take a series of grandfather clocks and place them on the same wall, the pendulum motion of the weights will move at different rates. If you close the door and come back several days later, the weights will all be swinging together. They will have synchronized themselves through a principle known as sympathetic vibrational resonance.

Some form of sympathetic vibrational resonance seems to be at work everywhere. Oysters on the East Coast of North America open and close at particular times according to some relationship with the cycles of the moon. Take one of those oysters, carry it in a sealed container to the center of the United States, and it will still open and close to East Coast rhythms — even if kept in total darkness. After living together for a few months, the menstrual cycles of female college roommates and military nurses who share dormitories will tend to cluster around the same time of the month — there is a synchronization of the periodic cycle of their menses. High-speed films taken of mothers and newborns show that they spend a significant amount of time mirroring each other's facial expressions and actions — a synchronization that is apparently essential for the healthy physical and physiological development of the babies.

Our connection to larger forces does not stop with synchronization, either. Subtle cues from our environment help form the very substance of our bodies and the conditions of our experience, as experiments with stem cells shows.[4] Stem cells are found in embryos and are uniquely adaptable — having the capacity to differentiate into specific cell types. Some will become brain cells; some will become liver cells, and so on. Now there is evidence that this capacity is not limited solely to embryonic development. When stem cells isolated from the brains of mice are injected into the blood streams of mature mice, the cells develop into blood cells — an adaptation not driven by genetic programming. In other words, the stem cells appear to pick up cues from their local environment in response to which they change their very function.

Our capacity to adapt to change is a function of our ability to attune ourselves to the fundamental waves of coherence that are broadcast through the universe.

We are embedded in organized energy — a view that is supported by breakthroughs in cosmology, biology, whole systems theory, chaos theory, and quantum mechanics. Many cultures have understood the mechanism of this direct connection to the fundamental rhythms of life.

Three mesas rise out of the multi-colors of the Painted Desert in northern Arizona, site of Old Orabai, the oldest continuously inhabited settlement in the Americas and home to the Hopi. They will tell you that they have been guided to these mesas by the will of the Creator.[5] Old Orabai has been around since well before the first Europeans stepped foot on this land, and the Hopi trace their ancestry back not only through the history of this continent but through a series of Earth changes which are faithfully recounted in the story of their migrations. Their survival is linked to a complex series of rituals, dances, and ceremonies by which they establish a connection to the non-human world. That connection maintains their spiritual lives and provides them the skills and conditions necessary to grow corn where it shouldn't really grow.

A friend of mine, invited to a number of Hopi rituals, was given several ears of their corn as part of his invitation. He took the corn back to his home near Los Angeles, planted it, and watered it regularly. To his astonishment it grew nearly 16 feet high and produced ears that were extraordinarily large. When he invited several Hopi elders to come and see, one turned to the others and exclaimed, "See what happens when you water our corn!" That corn was developed not by some agribusiness chemist but by a sacred reciprocal relationship between the Hopi and the natural world.

Hopi prophecies, handed down from clan leader to clan leader for many generations, have correctly predicted men talking through cobwebs (telephones), a gourd of ashes from the sky (the atomic bomb), a house of mica (the United Nations), roads in the sky (air travel routes), and moving houses of iron (trucks and automobiles). The prophecies also predicted that red hats from the East would meet them carrying truth in their hearts. A group of displaced Tibetan teachers had a formal meeting with the Hopi several years ago — teachers from a sect of Buddhism known for its red hats.

The Hopi remind us that it is possible to achieve resonance with some of the hidden cycles and larger fields of energy in our world. We are being challenged to consider the many cycles of life — from our heartbeats to the movements of the moon — that connect us to a larger and more meaningful whole. We are being asked to open our hearts and minds to the reality of that connection and to live in ways that can support it.

What are the behaviors that limit connection, and what are the behaviors that enhance it? Rigid time constraints, deadlines, and clocks interfere with our capacity to respond to natural cycles. It is nearly a cultural cliché that First Nations people are always bumping up against Euro-derived conceptions of time. But Westerners, with their conviction that events happen (and ought to happen) within a distinct time frame, also bump up against First Nations concepts of time, as anyone who has attended a First Nations ceremony or participated in a First Nations celebration could attest. And Westerners suffer the loss — true ceremony opens time and reveals a fluidity that invites a deeper participation in life.

I have experienced Native time most directly at times of birth and death. When a birth is close the normal constraints of everyday time are put aside, and attention fixes on the cycles of rhythmic pulsation known as labor. A timeless presence begins to permeate and touch the lives of those attending the birth. A similar timelessness accompanies the dying process. The usual business of life is put aside as people tend to the closing of another cycle of existence. Time slows down and the eternal becomes palpable.

We need to restore a sacred dimension to time. Our tendency to believe we can live outside the larger cycles of nature leads us to create strategies of domination and control that are not in keeping with the nested nature of interdependent systems. Contact with the natural world awakens a direct experience of what it means to live cyclically. Nature is a powerful antidote to despair and fear and offers us a direct way by which we can attune our bodies to cosmic cycles. A few extra minutes each day spent gazing up at the stars can do much to help restore an immediate and sensory experience of cyclic phenomena. Tracking the changes of the moon, sun, tides, and seasons can also help reinforce our awareness of larger cycles.

For those who cannot easily access the natural world, try setting your internal clocks to the periods of the day. Many monastic traditions throughout the world call people to prayer in a rhythm that moves elegantly through the daily cycles of light and dark. If you can find a way to pause at sunrise, midday, sunset, and in the depth of night you can begin to set your internal clock to larger rhythms. It may seem a simple task in the face of global change, but such a re-synchronization can have large-scale results. We return — come home to a sense of our place in the consciously unfolding universe. We release our reliance on the surfaces of life. Each day becomes a temple in which we seek what is true, good, and eternal.

Notes

1. See A.E. Gill, *Atmosphere-Ocean Dynamics* (Academic Press, 1982). Also see J.R. Apel, *Principles of Ocean Physics* (Academic Press, 1987). For information on the Internet, see http://www.pikpotsdam.de/~stefan/home_11.tm

2. See Edward R. Dewey and Mandino Og, Cycles: *The Mysterious Forces That Trigger Events* (Hawthorn Books, 1971).

3. See Maurice M. Cotterell, *The Mayan Prophecies* (Element, 1995).

4. See http://www.theraed.com/library/articles/stemcells.htm and http://www.alssurvivalguide.com/alsnewe/000419embryonicbreakthroughs.htm for information on stem cell search.

5. See Frank Waters and Oswald White Bear Fredericks, *Book of the Hopi* (Viking, 1985).

Additional Resources

INTERNET LINKS

http://www.climate.unbibe.ch/~christof/div/fact4thc.html
Fact sheet on thermohaline cycles by Christof Appenzeller, Department of Climate and Environmental Physics, University of Bern.

http://www.agu.org/revgeophys/schmit01/schmit01.html
The ocean component of the global water cycle by Raymond W. Schmitt, Department of Physical Oceanography, Woods Hole Oceanographic Institution, Woods Hole, Massachusetts.

http://www.cycles.org/cycles.htm
The Foundation for the Study of Cycles.

http://www.circadian.org/biothyt.html
Web site of the Circadian Rhythm Laboratory.

http://www.sfu.ca/~mcantle/rhythms.html
Simon Fraser University Circadian Rhythms Laboratory.

http://www.halfmoon.org/calfork.html
Mayan Calendar Site. A good beginning point; easily accessible.

http://www.mayanmajix.com/index.html
An excellent overview of research on the Mayan Calendar.

http://pinto.mtwilson.edu/Education/Presentations/Sunspot_Cycle/
Mount Wilson Observatory's concise history of sunspots.

http://fusedweb.pppl.gov/CPEP/Chart_pages/5.Plasmas/SunLayers.html
An excellent overview of the dynamics of the sun presented by the Princeton
Plasma Physics Laboratory.

http://www.nas.edu/ssb/maxmenu.htm
A well-thought-out description of solar functioning.

BOOKS

Campbell, Paul D. *Astronomy and the Maya Calendar Correlation.* Aegean
Park Press, 1992. Mayan Studies Series, No. 5. ISBN 0894121944

Courlander, Harold, author; and Enrico Arno, illustrator. *The Fourth World of
the Hopis: The Epic Story of the Hopi Indians As Preserved in Their Legends
and Traditions.* University of New Mexico Press, 1987. ISBN 0826310117

Jacklet, Jon W., ed. *Neuronal and Cellular Oscillators.* Marcel Dekker, 1989.
ISBN 0824780302

Lekson, Stephen, John R. Stei, and Simon J. Ortiz. *Chaco Canyon: A Center
and Its World.* Museum of New Mexico Press, 1997. ISBN 0890132615

Noble, David Grant, ed. *New Light on Chaco Canyon.* School of American
Research Press, 1984. ISBN 0933452101

Waters, Frank and Oswald White Bear Fredericks. *Book of the Hopi.* Viking
Press, 1985. ISBN 0140045279

Note

The following books are available from the Foundation for the Study of Cycles at http://www.cycles.org/catalog.htm:

Dewey, Edward R. and Og Mandino. *Cycles: The Mysterious Forces That Trigger Events*. 1971. Covers the interrelationships of biological, geological, and astronomical cycles with those that are social, political, and psychological. The basic book on cycle theory.

Dewey, Edward R. and Edwin F. Dakin. *Cycles: The Science of Prediction*. 1964. A popular treatment of cycles that brings together much of the information on cycles in economics, biology, and astronomy.

Wilson, Louise L. *Catalogue of Cycles: Economics*. 1964. A collection of 1,380 cycle allegations in economic data. Indexes by author and wavelength; bibliography.

Interlude

THE STRETCHER-BEARER

In the trenches of World War I there was a stretcher-bearer
who, when faced with the horror of a world at war with itself,
was able to intuit a deeper message from the chaos.
Teilhard de Chardin, a Jesuit paleontologist, philosopher,
and mystic was to synthesize a vision of the spiritual potential
of matter itself. His work gave rise to the notion of the nooesphere
— now used to describe the network of ideas and communication
systems that encircle the globe. De Chardin is a good example
of someone who was able to move into the heart of chaos and
find the ground of invariant truths.

The night sky had been uneasy for days. It was always so
before an offensive. Our steel-throated guns spewed
forth fire, and from across the desolation between us and
the Germans a muted thunder answered. Close to the front
the ground, the surrounding countryside, even the shape
of our thoughts, seemed strange. I would have gone mad
in the horror if not for a stretcher-bearer I had met.

I was a runner — my job was to take messages between
the front and the safety of headquarters. I lived in two worlds.
Behind the front line the trees stood unmolested, and flowers

in the meadows bloomed untouched. You could hear the quiet of the Earth. Ahead in the mud and thunder of the front all that was jettisoned. In the trenches you could never settle down into the small habits and annoyances of life. Here there was a strange society of purpose, which had an enemy as its focus.

I hated that enemy until I met the stretcher-bearer. I literally ran into him one day as I was taking a message to a command post in one of the forward trenches. I turned the corner of the trench and hit him squarely on the run. We both fell into the mud. I reached out to give him a hand, apologizing over and over. His first comment will always stay with me. "It is good to have somewhere to go."

He wasn't angered; he wasn't upset. What he was, was observant. I have never met a man who was more observant, so able to see to the heart of things. It was his vision that endeared him to me. Where I saw bloodshed, bitterness, and the cruelty of war he was able to see beyond and through all difficulty.

No one in our regiment was braver; no one served with a more diligent attention to detail; no one stayed up longer or worked more extra hours than he did. He risked his life again and again. And never once, from the time he joined our regiment in January of 1915 until the end of the war, was he ever wounded or even sick.

Once when we were walking together behind the lines, I saw him fall to his knees just to study a stone. He held it up to the light and ran his fingers carefully over its surfaces, as if he were trying to read the pattern of matter as a language. Watching him that day in the blessed silence of the field, I saw a man who could see light in the very earth under his feet.

"Nothing is profane for one who truly sees," he said. That comment made in a university lecture hall or in some boisterous cafe in Paris would probably not mean much. Just one more idea in a maze of ideas. But this man uttered these words at the margin of carnage. And he uttered them after having risked his life many times to bring back the wounded from the terrible acreage called "no-man's-land." Let me tell you, after you've lived for days and weeks in the refuge of the mud you feel mighty naked scaling the trench, facing bullets and bombs. There is no greater doorway a man must go through than to rise up in the face of death and reach out to save another. When my friend said, "Nothing is profane for one who truly sees," he spoke as one who had been inside the belly of war.

"How can you see beyond the blood?" I once asked him when he came back drenched in the blood of a soldier that he had carried to safety.

"I don't see beyond it." A pause let me know that was his answer.

"I don't understand," I replied, ducking involuntarily as the whine of an incoming round filled the air.

"I don't see beyond it," he replied. "I see into it. It is the Earth that bleeds. It is all mankind that bleeds. I do not want to turn away from such a sight, for I believe that there is a purpose to all that happens. I will know more of that purpose if I look into the reality before me."

They offered him promotion out of the trenches, but he always turned it down. He wanted to stay with the men. When I asked him why, he said, "To serve something greater than oneself, that is one of the lessons of this terrible conflict. I have no greater way of honoring my Maker than to serve those who struggle so." I didn't even know he was a priest then. I always knew he was good, a fine and true man.

One day when the two of us were taking a break far beyond the noise of the guns, he looked up from the paper he was writing on and said, "There will come a time when the whole world will understand the meaning of unity." How could he say such a thing when day after day we had been carrying the dead and wounded out of the trenches? How could he say such a thing?

When I asked him, he said, "We fight from our ignorance, not from our wisdom. But when you strip away the colors of our clothing, the shapes of our helmets, you see the same human urge to transcend our condition. This is what this war is about. It is about the triumph of spirit through matter. This clash of opposites is the meeting place of humanity searching for a new resolution." I thought him a bit strange when he said that. But later when I was to read his books and absorb his thoughts in the tranquillity of more peaceful times, I came to understand that he truly saw such a possibility.

Because of him I learned not to hate our enemy, and joined with him in the work of serving those who were in need. And sometimes at sunset when the sky was bright with amazing color, I tried to look beyond the trenches — as he did so often — and see the light in this world of ours.

Chapter Seven

Paradigm Shifts, Strange Attractors, and Chaos

IN THE 1960s meteorologist Edward Lorenz created a computer program to simulate weather change. His machine was large and unwieldy, and it kept breaking down. But it worked — he was able to create his own weather simulations from a handful of mathematical formulations.

One day Lorenz decided to use a shortcut. He wanted to examine a particular sequence in greater detail, but instead of starting over he typed in values from an earlier printout and began the computational run in mid-sequence. Then he went down the hall to get a cup of coffee while the vacuum tubes and wires did their work. When he came back he discovered that the new printout bore no resemblance to the old.

Lorenz was mystified. What could have made such a difference to the two printouts? After considerable effort he discovered that he had rounded one of the numbers in the first printout from 0.506127 to 0.506 to save space. The computer had the original figure in its memory, but the new run was launched on the shortened value. A thousandth of a difference in value should not have made such a difference in outcome, but it did. In fact the outcome was so different that Lorenz was forced to think in new ways to account for it.

Rather than throw away the outcome as an annoying anomaly, Lorenz realized he had stumbled on evidence that showed — in one way at least — how a small change can bring about large-scale transformations. More importantly he realized that his discovery was a key to understanding the patterns of chaos. Over the next few years Lorenz's work helped launched a new science — chaos theory — and his few moments of inattention ended up changing our concepts of causality.[1]

Lorenz is not the only scientist whose work has helped trigger a paradigm shift. On a Christmas night in 1642 a newborn child was struggling for his life. In the sky above a comet could be seen, and those who contemplated the heavens wondered what manner of catastrophe was being predicted. The child, who was not expected to survive, went on to live past 80 and, in the course of his life, changed history. Isaac Newton — for he was the child — was determined to show that celestial objects obeyed strict natural laws of motion rather than the arbitrary dictates of some mysterious heavenly force. Working in the late 1600's, and over several years of an almost monk-like existence, Newton wrote the *Philosophiae Naturalis Principia Mathematica* — possibly the single most influential scientific book ever written; in it Newton presented a coherent view of how the universe works based on causality. His discoveries helped transform the science and technology of his times and created a legacy of "cause and effect" thinking that propelled Western models — scientific, political, commercial, and philosophical — toward the mechanistic (some would say with catastrophic results).

In one of the great ironies of history, sophisticated versions of a calculating machine invented by a rival mathematician are helping to unseat Newtonian determinism. Chaos theory requires computers to model and track the complex phenomena being investigated. Newton's bitterest rival, Gottfried Wilhelm Leibnitz, (the two fought over who was the true originator of calculus) developed the binary mathematics that was to lead to modern computer science, and invented one of the first working calculating machines in the Western world.

Regardless of the age in which we live, we all seem to want to exert control over change. Ancient cultures attributed responsibility to some agency beyond human understanding for changes they had to contend with. Isaac Newton's need to establish order in the heavens may well have been influenced by the disorder that surrounded him. (Fatherless and abandoned by his mother when he was three Newton became secretive, suspicious, and controlling, waging long battles with those he thought had wronged him. Plague broke out in London just as he finished a significant portion of his schooling, and he fled to the countryside. A year later the Great London Fire gutted much of the city, making his return to it even more problematic.) Some 300 years after Newton, Lorenz wanted to create models of natural events that would help him predict the weather. Modern chaos theory coupled with quantum mechanics opens the door to another option — the recognition and acceptance of change and a certain amount of chaos as essential for the overall health of all systems.

Perhaps at this point a short course in chaos theory is in order.[2] Chaos theory suggests that turbulence and change are constantly dancing around the edges of stability. Within the stable world of demonstrated cause and effect is a stream of possibility verging on chaos — a creative edge that mediates differing layers of reality from atomic vibration to the movement of galaxies. Within these boundary layers, where chaos often occurs, small changes can bring about large-scale shifts. Think of the human body. While the overall integrity of the body is maintained, at molecular and cellular levels there is a seething sea of vibration and change as cells are made and remade over the course of a person's lifetime. The red spot on Jupiter — a phenomenon that has been observed for several hundred years — is, in fact, an eddy that has maintained its integrity in the gaseous winds of the planet that nearly became a sun.

Chaos theorists conceptualize various patterns of events as particular types of attractors. Imagine a stream of water coming from a faucet. At a low rate of flow the stream falls in a straight line toward the ground; as the flow increases it begins to swing back and forth like a pendulum. (In chaos terms, this is known as a point attractor.)

An example of a limit attractor can be found in the flow of a water flushing toilet. The rising level of water triggers a floating mechanism which shuts off the incoming water at a certain point. This feedback between level and input creates a limit which acts as a way to organize the system.

As water flow increases the pendulum action changes, beginning to swing in a circle (known as a torus attractor). Kayakers who have ridden the dome of a strong eddy and found themselves pushed above the level of the surrounding water have experienced the effects of a torus attractor firsthand. Torus attractors can also be visualized by considering the ubiquitous bagel. Everyday events tend to loop in repeating patterns, though they never repeat in exactly the same way. If you could graph those patterns, actions that are very similar would cluster and form the center of the torus (the bagel hole); actions that are dissimilar — the variations — would spread out and form the circumference of the torus (the bagel).

The next stage in chaos evolution is not as easy to visualize. When torus attractors break down strange attractors appear. Twists, leaps, reverses, skips, and other very strange behaviors characterize these attractors — hence the name "strange." In one of the most well-known strange attractors — the butterfly attractor — patterns of events trace wing-like paths that link together in the "body" of the butterfly.

In speaking of the cascade from order to chaos, theoreticians talk about strange attractors producing domain basins — the probable area in which the flow of events will gather. Think of a ball bearing rolling around in a large bowl. Eventually it will come to rest at the bottom of the bowl, creating a stable domain basin. In a complex system many attractors will be competing to become the final domain basin.

Two other aspects of chaos theory are pertinent to our discussion. First, stable attractors resist change. If an attractor's basin boundary is destroyed — think sides of a bowl — it is called a crisis. Second, as a system moves in increasingly unpredictable ways, events branch at various points — called bifurcations — creating ever-more-elaborate patterns.

So what does all this theory have to do with real life?[3] Well, we can draw some interesting parallels between the two. First, we could say that we are already familiar with point and limit attractors. The flow of such things as industrial goods, services, medicines, and money can be thought of as streams of water — stable as long as they do not overwhelm the structures through which they move. And what happens when the structures break down? We make all kinds of attempts to create new structures. In chaos terms we go through a crisis: new attractors appear as the old ones collapse. New domain basins are created and destroyed until, finally, a new stability is established.

Second, we could say we are also familiar with torus attractors. Our habitual patterns of behavior and ways of seeing and interpreting the world can be thought of as repeating and self-referential — like a torus (think bagel again). (If our focus of attention constantly refers back to ourselves we are caught in a torus attractor.) While stable, those patterns can easily become rigid and restricting.

As we develop the capacity to see and act beyond our often-narrow view of things, we can break the hold of the torus attractors that impede us from functioning fully. Nearly every spiritual tradition speaks of the necessity of going beyond obsessive self-interest and toward service. Service to something greater than one's self purifies and leads to spiritual maturity, allowing butterfly wing and other strange attractors to emerge.

Third, we could say that we know something about strange attractors and may even be intuitively drawn to them. Though they sometimes create less-than-desirable effects, strange attractors are more adaptable than torus attractors — an appealing characteristic in times that call for flexibility. (Remember, they emerge when torus attractors break down.) They have enough structure to maintain overall performance and enough novelty to produce new and different forms of expression.

Strange attractors have made themselves felt throughout history. Just prior to the Industrial Revolution there was an upsurge in the food supply in England. The torus attractor of food collection and distribution was disturbed, and suddenly there was enough labor to allow for the creation of a butterfly attractor. One wing collected food, and the other went about the business of making new things.

After the first few months of deadly trench warfare during World War I, Christmas Day, 1914, dawned bright and cold, freezing the sea of mud between the enemies. Allied and Axis soldiers spilled out of the trenches and spontaneously gathered in the middle of no-man's-land, exchanging gifts, playing soccer, and re-discovering their common humanity. Reacting in horror at the implications of such behavior, the generals forbade further fraternization under the threat of death. And so the war continued. But for one moment in the midst of all that anger, hatred, and violence a new force emerged. A strange attractor — love — took over and transformed reality.

Today, tourism represents a strange attractor that reconfigures the world by effectively erasing some of the borders that previously kept people in isolation from one another. The planes, trains, cars, hotels, and restaurants maintained by the travel industry are linked in a worldwide network that exhibits remarkable stability. Yet new experiences — twists, turns, and leaps of fate, if you will — can appear for those who travel. The exposure to new cultures, different languages, foods, customs, and art can induce new perceptions and insights, which in turn can lead to yet more new experiences.

While we are on the subject of strange attractors we need to stay aware that when conventional systems undergo stress, hidden attractors can appear, too, and become powerful agents of change. Like archetypes, some hidden attractors create negative effects; some create positive effects. (Archetypes are hidden, implicit structures of energy that influence external events in powerful ways. The archetype of "The Great Mother," found throughout all histories and cultures, is the implicit pattern out of which all manifestations of mothering emerge, independent of any individual mother. In Jungian psychology one of the goals of the psychotherapeutic process is to help constellate and make known those archetypes that are affecting a person's behavior.) As we survey change we would be wise to learn to distinguish among attractors. The rise of Nazism and Gandhi's elaboration of nonviolence are two modern-day examples of hidden attractors that emerged in response to systemic stress. Nazism inflicted enormous physical and spiritual suffering on the world; nonviolence liberated a country.

Fourth, we could say that we know quite a bit about how a crisis affects stable attractors. Remember that in chaos terms, as boundary basins are destroyed, stable attractors resist change by trying to maintain their old patterns. In structures that organize around deterministic constructs of causality, the desire to exert complete control becomes epidemic. Viewed over several hundred years, strategies of control implicit in the structures of monarchy, feudalism, slavery, patriarchy, and organized religion have been or are being eroded by the dynamics of change in the stream of history. As global change accelerates we should expect to see a tightening in any of these structures that remain as they shift to resist change. And, indeed, I think we are seeing it with the emergence of the new conservatism, anti-feminist backlash, and an increased fundamentalism in both politics and religion.

Whether we look at the fine points or at the overall picture, chaos theory speaks to a continuous and necessary breakdown of order. At the edge of chaos old constructs and the power of accurate prediction fall apart as new possibilities explode in many dimensions. In our personal lives, when we change the boundary conditions of our experiences, unexpected outcomes occur. Death, birth, disease, shifting relationships, travel, and new learning experiences are boundary changes that induce transformation.

At this point in history our cultural boundary basins are undergoing rapid modification. We could choose to perceive these changes as catastrophic. But if we take a longer view, those same changes have implicit within them the hint of a larger order. Our challenge as a culture is to restructure our understanding of change and find new ways of adapting to shifting environments. These adaptations will be best served by cultivating diversity, by encouraging an open exchange of information, by developing pattern recognition, and by learning to recognize emerging attractors.

The list that follows is made up of verified theorems of chaos theory. The theorems are, in large part, derived mathematically and describe very precise technical processes. The analogies and short commentaries on how the truths of chaos theory manifest in our individual and cultural experiences are my creations.

Chaos Theory: As change accelerates, the possible outcomes reach a point where normal cause and effect break down.

Analogy: The ultimate seduction of Western rationalism is the belief that we can somehow organize correctly, function well enough, and problem-solve sufficiently to mitigate impending crises. As change accelerates old patterns and strategies of behaviour will simply stop working. That breakdown will affect those patterns found in the external world but also those that exist in our internal thought processes. To develop empathy for others try embodying their point of view and see what you can learn — especially those you have the most difficulty with. Be willing to risk your own point of view, too. Radical solutions will take us further than stopgap methods. Be ready for the unexpected.

Chaos Theory: Certainty and control become unstable in a developing field of chaos.

Analogy: Fixed ideas and attachment to specific outcomes will not work in the face of overwhelming change. As individuals or in a group we must pay attention to the gestalt of meaning — both content and context — in any given situation and be willing to move in directions that may appear nonsensical to us at first. This expanded way of seeing holds that the gaps between one's thoughts are as important as the thoughts themselves, and that open spaces are as important as the objects that exist within them.

Chaos Theory: Multiple realities, simultaneous points of view, and different worlds all may exist within the same time and space.

Analogy: There is no single correct way of approaching complex systems and their interactions in the world, though the art of listening is a most desirable skill. The construct of reality we co-inhabit can have multiple realities contained within it (as any public meeting will dramatically confirm), and there will be many solutions and many failures, all of which will be being generated by the same global transition. Multiple realities inform each other, fertilize, stimulate, and stir the cauldron of creativity.

Chaos Theory: After a certain stage of bifurcation, event basins appear which are the domains of the outcome.

Analogy: Some time after the predictable world begins to change, distinct areas of possible outcomes begin to appear that are influenced by the quality of our intention. If we collapse into fear we will land in a fearful event basin. If we increase our creative capacity we will join a basin with a potential for more positive outcomes. We have choices about where we align our energies. In a field of highly charged intention the map of new domains becomes highly fluid, so we need to appeal to the feel of the flow between us and be alert to what may be emergent beyond our limited points of view.

Chaos Theory: Systems in a state of disequilibrium can become highly sensitive to new information, experiment profusely, and adapt quickly.

Analogy: Experimentation, creative thinking, new ideas, and risk-taking are essential responses for the emergence of solutions. When traditional structures of feedback and control begin to fray, solutions appear where before there were only obstacles. With the collapse of the Soviet Union an economy that hybridizes elements of socialism, capitalism, crime, and barter has emerged in Russia. One company has a staff of 50 people whose sole job is to arrange complex barters with other companies all across the country. A friend of mine who was in Moscow during the collapse still marvels at the ingenuity she saw exhibited there. She reported that people actually seemed to like the challenge of creating new ways of coping.

Chaos Theory: A system on the edge of chaos is sensitively dependent on initial conditions.

Analogy: Actions taken now — even small, seemingly inconsequential ones — can have huge effects later on. Our commitment to this discussion, for instance, has the potential to engender wide-scale change that is beyond our capacity to envision right now. One or two seed ideas formed within the focus of our work here may have the power to bring enormous change in the external world. We should never underestimate the power of local actions to affect the wider field.

When initial conditions are disturbed unpredictable outcomes occur. When the Black Death appeared and spread over most of Europe (carried on the backs of rats), an interesting ancillary effect occurred. So many people died that the wealth tended to be concentrated in the hands of the remaining few, giving rise to a new class that had — for the first time in hundreds of years — the economic clout to challenge the privilege of royalty. Some say that modern democracy was born during this period of economic adjustment. The attractor of the feudal class system shifted at the onset of plague, with unforeseen results. A disease carried by the tiniest creatures — fleas — led to the restructuring of human culture.

Chaos Theory: In chaos diagrams, no point or patterns of points ever recur in exactly the same way, and yet there is a new kind of order that can be seen if the scale of observation is large enough.

Analogy: What appears as chaos may, in fact, be evidence of a larger order or a grander sweep of history, and we may need to experiment with our tolerance levels for disorder as new forms emerge. When data from a recent study of 1.2 million teenage pregnancies was plotted on a conventional timeline, it had too much "noise" to reveal any clear-cut pattern. When the same statistics were analyzed using mathematics derived from chaos theory, a pattern emerged showing that these events were being constellated in ways that social research scientists still don't understand.[4] What was clear, however, was that teen pregnancies were occurring in patterns inaccessible to conventional analytical methods.

When surveying change we may sometimes need to reserve judgment for a while. No two snowflakes or leaves are ever the same, but no one would deny they are ordered entities. Sometimes individual dots on paper resolve into pictures if you stand back far enough. A deeper field of resonance and coherence may be operating that is far beyond our current comprehension of social change.

Weather patterns, animal populations, environmental conditions, economies, technologies, and political systems are some of the complex systems showing signs of increased stress as change continues to accelerate. We can contract in fear and try to exert control over forces we do not understand, denying that domain basins of magnificence lurk just beyond our unease. Or we can hold to the philosopher's stone and search for new possibilities in the heart of chaos. New networks of ideas, cooperation, and technologies; new business practices; a redistribution of political power; more compassionate action; and a healthy, more livable planet may be the outcome.

Isaac Newton spent his life struggling to find order in the universe. One wonders what might have happened to the history of science and of the world if there had been a bit more kindness and compassion in his personal life. Would an open heart have helped move him beyond mere determinism? We have an opportunity to discover the answer to that question.

Notes

1. See Michael R.A. Williams, *A History of Computing Technology* (Prentice-Hall, 1985). For more information on the history of computers, see Stan Augarten, *Bit by Bit: An Illustrated History of Computers* (Ticknor and Fields, 1984). Also see Chronology of Digital Computing Machines to 1952. http://www.best.com /~wilson/faq/chrono.html

2. See James Gleick, *Making a New Science* (Penguin, 1987) and Ian Stewart, *Does God Play Dice? The Mathematics of Chaos* (Penguin, 1989). For information on chaos theory on the Internet, see http://www.imho.com/grae/chaos/chaos.html

3. See http://www.tryoung.com for a site linking chaos theory and human action.

4. See T.R. Young, *"Chaos Theory and Causality in Complex Social Dynamics"*, The Red Feather Institute

Additional Resources

INTERNET LINKS

http://wwwimho.com/grae/chaos/chaos.html
A good introductory essay to Chaos Theory, with illustrations by Gregory Rae. Easy and readable.

http://library.thinkquest.org/3493/
A survey of Chaos Theory.

http://order.ph.utexas.edu/chaos/
An on-line course on Chaos Theory for the lay person by Dr. Matthew A. Trump; Ilya Prigogine Center for Studies in Statistical Mechanics and Complex Systems, University of Texas at Austin.

http://xyz.lanl.gov/archive/nlin/
A source for highly technical papers on nonlinear systems by the Los Alamos Center for Nonlinear Studies.

http://www.tryoung.com/chaos/chaosindex.html
Some of the best papers on chaos theory and real-world situations by T.R. Young.

http://www.haven.net/patterns/news.html
Interesting applications of chaos theory to educational issues by the *Systems Thinking and Chaos Theory Network Newsletter.*

BOOKS

Briggs, John, and David F. Peat. *Seven Life Lessons of Chaos: Timeless Wisdom from the Science of Change.* Harper Collins, 1999. ISBN 0060182466

———*Turbulent Mirror: An Illustrated Guide to Chaos Theory and the Science of Wholeness.* Harper Collins, 1990. ISBN 0060916966

Gleick, James. *Chaos: Making a New Science.* Penguin USA, 1988. ISBN 0140092501

Hall, Nina, ed. *Exploring Chaos: A Guide to the New Science of Disorder.* W. W. Norton, 1994. ISBN 0393312267

Holland, John H., author; and Heather Mimnaugh, editor. *Hidden Order: How Adaptation Builds Complexity.* Perseus Press, 1996. ISBN 0201442302

Kauffman, Stuart. *At Home in the Universe: The Search for Laws of Self-Organization and Complexity.* Oxford University Press, 1996. ISBN 0195111303

Leibniz, Gottried Wilhelm, author; and G.H.R. Parkinson, editor. *Philosophical Writings.* Everyman Paperback Classics, 1997. ISBN 0460875469

Lorenz, Edward N. *The Essence of Chaos.* University of Washington Press, 1996. The Jessie and John Danz Lecture Series. ISBN 0295975148

Stewart, Ian. *Does God Play Dice? The Mathematics of Chaos.* Blackwell, 1990. ISBN 1557861064

Waldrop, M. Mitchell. *Complexity: The Emerging Science at the Edge of Order and Chaos.* Touchstone Books, 1993. ISBN 0671872346

Westfall, Richard S. *Never at Rest: A Biography of Isaac Newton.* Cambridge University Press, 1983. ISBN 0521274354

White, Michael. *Isaac Newton: The Last Sorcerer.* Perseus Books, 1999. ISBN 073820143X

A Menorah at Trinity

*We turn here to Robert Oppenheimer, who was
instrumental in the development of the atomic bomb.
The moment the first bomb was detonated at
Trinity, war and the potential for the extinction of
life on this planet became inextricably bound.
I have put words to parts of Oppenheimer's life
story in order that we may consider the problem of
judgment, power, and human aggression.*

They say that I have cancer of the throat. My voice will be stricken soon, so I must speak now if I am to speak at all. And what is there to say? I could speak of the days early in the war when we wrestled to make a dream come true in the crisp air of New Mexico. I could speak of the intensity of those hours and days, of the pressure that forced its way into our lives, bringing divorce and making enemies out of the closest of friends. I could even talk about the light that was born that day at Trinity, a light so odd that I hope never to see its like again.

"I have been Death, Destroyer of Worlds," I whispered as the bomb ignited before our unbelieving eyes.

I am not sure why, of all the words that might arise at such a moment, the *Bhagavad Gita* should come to mind. Perhaps it was the battlefield setting — so similar to the plain of Kurukshetra where Krishna revealed his divine nature to Arjuna. Or perhaps it was because in that ancient document the identification of good and evil is so very precise.

I have not lived such a precise life. I have gone from hero to villain and back again. Hailed as a savior of the nation for my work on the atom bomb. Reviled as a communist sympathizer and denied the opportunity to help guide the very power I had helped unleash. Perhaps Krishna was right when he counseled Arjuna to not be caught in the snares of either praise or blame. Perhaps, but that is not what I want to talk about today.

I wish to speak of the desert yucca. It was that simple plant I remember more than even the terrible light of Trinity. The yucca looked a bit like a menorah, hands upraised toward the heavens, as if it were waiting patiently for human foolishness to be at an end. In the middle of its sharpened lances was a lone delicate flower. I do not practice the religion of my people, but I saw the eye of the Creator in that single yucca flower. I saw in one brief moment that the delicate beauty of one flower could outshine the raging power of a sun.

My throat begins to tire, so I must choose my words
carefully. What I have to say is about intelligence. There are
those who thought me a genius, and I must admit that there
was a time when the power of my mind enthralled me. I may
have been intelligent enough to grope my way into the secrets
of the atom — and groping was all any of us was doing in
those years — but I was not wise enough to take a true
measure of the human hearts of those around me.

Friends and colleagues called me traitor because I spoke
against developing the terrible weapon of the hydrogen bomb.
I saw no need to create the kind of force that could be
unleashed by such a device; an atomic explosion was enough.
So I argued with the awakening force of moral outrage against
creating any more man-made suns.

I spoke from my conscience, and my enemies twisted my
words against me. I was led into a trap at the hearing on
my security clearance and made to look like a liar and a cheat.
This was the thanks I received for helping to end the war.

But I am forgetting the wisdom of the yucca flower and
the beauty of its light. And my throat has allowed me to say
about all that I can. There is a power that is greater than us all.
I was not a praying man, but after that day at Trinity I prayed
for us to awaken and abandon the pursuit of absolute power
that is so very much our obsession.

Oppenheimer was honored again by the American government near the end of his life, but he never fully recovered from the blow to his spirit at the hands of his own people. He died of throat cancer, joining the ranks of many others who also succumbed to some form of cancer after working on the bomb.

Chapter Eight

MISSING ENERGY, SPEEDING STARS, AND THE POWER OF LOVE

And yet to me what is this quintessence of dust?

— *Hamlet* Act II, scene ii

O<small>N AN</small> O<small>CTOBER NIGHT</small> in 1923, a man was examining the stars. As a child, this man had consumed books on science fiction, travel, and adventure, and Jules Verne's writing had inspired him to believe in the unseen, the impossible, and the unknown. Even so the man nearly didn't make his appointment with destiny. Before becoming an astronomer he had been a Rhodes scholar studying law. He couldn't shake the allure of the unknown, however, and quit his studies to devote himself to astronomy. Then World War I intervened and his academic career was temporarily halted. He joined in the fight, and in fact, apparently liked to fight. He became an accomplished boxer and was urged to turn professional. This man's tenacity and willingness to stay with an opponent was to transfer to his scientific work, for it took him nearly ten years to tease out of the night sky the secrets that would make him famous.

On a photograph taken that night in October, 1923, the man circled a particular star and scrawled the abbreviation "VAR" around it — identifying a cephaid variable star that was clearly located beyond our own galaxy. Edwin Hubble had just discovered proof that the universe is expanding. His study of the motion of galaxies was to usher in a radical new cosmology, the principles of which are still being elaborated by scientists who study the fascinating inner workings of the universe.[1]

According to the Big Bang theory — one of the precepts of the new cosmology — the universe is the result of an instantaneous and spontaneous emergence of time, space, matter, and light. Contrary to our common understanding of explosions emerging out of one thing and into another, the Big Bang did not have a universe to emerge out of — the Big Bang is the universe. All that we see, encounter, observe, and seek to understand emerged as a result of that torrid cosmic event.

Though the debate is still a lively and contentious issue among cosmologists, thus far scientists have developed three models to describe the shape of the universe.[2] In the open universe model the expansion of galaxies continues unabated. In the closed universe model gravitational forces will eventually draw all matter back together toward a single conflagration. And in the flat universe model a gradually slowing expansion will level off, ultimately creating a nearly steady state.

The Big Bang left a calling card from the beginning of time — a faint background glow of microwave radiation called the "cosmic micro background" (CMB). New measurements of the CMB suggest that the universe is operating in ways that are most consistent with the flat model (based on data from two microwave telescopes at the South Pole that scanned the subtle variations in this background field in 1998). If that new experimental evidence holds it means that something — most likely an unknown form of energy/matter exchange — is pushing against the contractile force of gravity.

Another line of inquiry suggests that the expansion of the universe is actually speeding up. Two different observatories have announced they have found evidence that, based on conventional cosmological equations, some distant supernovas are actually moving faster than they should.

And astronomers studying the rotation of galaxies have discovered a curious anomaly. Conventional wisdom says that as you move further from the center of a galaxy its rotation should slow down. What the astronomers have found, however, is that rotation remains constant throughout the radius of the galaxy. The only way to account for this unexpected result is to posit a form of matter that can't currently be seen.

All three sets of evidence point to the probability that some version of Einstein's repudiated Cosmological Constant is an actuality. (Edwin Hubble's discovery seemed to challenge the validity of the Cosmological Constant, and by the time the notion of the Big Bang had evolved into accepted theory, Einstein believed the Constant was the biggest mistake he ever made.) In considering the workings of the universe, Einstein reasoned that if its mass is constant and gravitation is factored in, it should be shrinking, creating a whirlpool into which we would all disappear. In his era, though, the universe was believed to be static, so Einstein introduced the Cosmological Constant as a hypothetical force that could counteract the contraction brought about by gravitational pull.

Einstein's mistake may have turned out to be true. Not only is the universe expanding, but there is also a force at work that is acting against gravity. Scientists now say that at least seventy percent — and possibly up to ninety percent — of the universe is made up of "dark matter/energy" that we cannot see.[3] ("Quintessence" is the most interesting form of dark energy thus far proposed. Posited as an entirely new field of energy, light passes through it uninterrupted and without refraction, making quintessence transparent and very difficult to find.) Furthermore, whatever is out there seems to be adding energy into the system so that the expansion of the universe is speeding up. So what is going on?

Two hypotheses are of interest for what they can tell us about energy and the makeup of the universe. One hypothesis hads it roots in a childhood experience of physicist David Bohm, who liked to wander from his small town and out into nature. One night he climbed a local hilltop and the light radiating from the town caught his attention. He suddenly understood that energy from the light reached out to the entire universe, as did his thoughts. All nature, he realized, is connected and made up of living energy.

Bohm took his childhood intuition and with a physicist's rigor developed an elegant hypothesis to help explain where the missing energy of the universe might be. According to his hypothesis empty space is not empty at all. Instead it is a vast sea of energy made up of quantized wave-like excitation upon which the material universe rests like a ripple on an underlying sea of activity. Fellow physicists scoffed at Bohm's notions, calling his sea of energy an illusion; but there is now experimental support for it, as shown by some recent research.[4]

The second hypothesis posits a kind of quantum soup in which particles jump in and out of existence in a continuous process of creation and annihilation that is essentially invisible to conventional methods of detection. In 1996 a cleverly designed experiment by Steven Lamoreaux at the University of Washington was able to measure the force of these quantum interactions, using a laser to measure the torsion on a pendulum from two specially prepared metal plates. The plates blocked the effect of other fields of energy while allowing any pressure created by quantum fluctuation to be measured. The force (now known as the Casimir effect) wasn't much, but it was measurable — about equivalent to the weight of a hemoglobin molecule compared to the weight of the Earth. Though not exactly Bohm's sea of energy, the Casimir effect does tell us the universe is more complicated than classical Newtonian physics would predict.

With the emergence of evidence of dark matter and quintessence, and the possibility that the Cosmological Constant is a reality, cosmological anomalies may be ushering in a new scientific era. We may, in fact, find ourselves in the same position as scientists found themselves near the end of the nineteenth century when physicists were describing reality in terms of the cause and effect principles laid down by Newton. (Nature was likened to a well-oiled machine.) Many scientists then felt they were very close to understanding all the workings of Nature. Then some peculiar experimental results were observed: light, which was known to act as a wave, was observed to be acting as if it were moving as discrete particles. (This photoelectric effect was one of the main avenues of investigation that led Einstein to his theory of relativity and was also integral to the development of quantum mechanics.) Classical physics and our understanding of how the world works was changed forever by the emergence of new, unexplained phenomenon. In their search for the missing energy of the universe, today's scientists may have to confront the limitations of their own worldview. Out of such paradox, great leaps of culture are made; I believe we are poised on the edge of another great leap.

To understand how quantum physics is changing our understanding of reality we can consult a map I playfully call "quantum coastlines."[5] Boundaries on the quantum map are not anything like the hard land/ocean margins we experience in our physical world. The more closely you examine the quantum coastline and the more detail you take in, the fuzzier the picture becomes. Like chaos theory, quantum theory can teach us something about how to deal with change.

First, according to quantum theory, you cannot simultaneously know your exact position and your speed: you have to sacrifice one for the other. In other words you cannot know much of who you are if you want to know where you are and vice versa — a difficult paradox. (The more we know where we are going, the less we know about ourselves. The more we know about ourselves, the less we know about where we are going.) The solution? The solution is found in our capacity to hold the tension of opposites. We get to know a little about who we are and a little about where we are going.

Second, events exist as probabilities and not as discrete occurrences. As we saw in chaos theory, outcomes are not predetermined and do not follow a definite sequence or path. Einstein, one of the better navigators of the quantum world in this century, was very annoyed at this part of the map. He tried to dismiss what he saw by saying, "God does not play dice with the universe."

Unfortunately for Einstein the evidence is overwhelming that, indeed, God does gamble — regularly and routinely. Indeterminacy is built-in to the fundamental structure of the universe. We can know the probability curve of an electron in motion, but we will never be able to capture the annoying little critter and put him in a display case. We are involved in a cosmic gamble, and in times of change the universe may just be rolling the dice to see if a new combination of numbers comes up with new outcomes and new possibilities.[6]

Third, particles act like waves and waves act like particles. This duality has been demonstrated experimentally for both light and matter. Our everyday experience with light helps us understand its wave-like nature: rainbows and the visual distortion of objects under water testify to this aspect of light. The green growing plants that sustain life on this planet attest to the particle nature of light: photosynthesis would not be possible if light could not enter plant cells as discrete particles.

Not only does light have a dual nature but so, too, does matter. We are used to thinking of matter as made up of particles — a pebble is a pebble not a rainbow — but at subatomic levels matter also appears as waves. Particle-wave duality, then, is embedded within the very matrix of reality.

If we were to draw a parallel between quantum theory and human behavior we could say that most of us tend to function with more ease in one realm than in the other. In times of stress some people will tend toward the concrete and discrete in their problem-solving; others will tend toward the more wave-like and diffuse.[7] It is essential that we try to master both realms as best we can and also attempt to open a dialogue between pebbles and rainbows. We cannot build foundations without stones, nor can we envision the elegance of an arch without rainbows.

Fourth, not only do waves and particles exchange natures, but they do so through objects. Imagine your hand approaching a barrier, suddenly smoothing out into a complex of waves that could pass through the lattice of matter, and reassembling itself as a hand on the other side. This may be just what we would like to have been able to do as children, but to be told as adults that dimensions of our world act in such ways is, to say the least, interesting. But at quantum levels of reality those kinds of shifts seem to be rather standard. Just as classical Newtonian physics was changed forever by the discovery of new, unexplained phenomena, so may discoveries in quantum physics usher in yet another shift in our worldview.

Science is poised at a doorway that could open into a realm familiar to those mystics and saints who say that consciousness is the prior reality out of which everything emerges. Thousands of years ago, adepts of the Indus Valley perfected techniques that allowed them to use their own mind/body interface as a lens for gazing into cosmological events.[8] They heard a vibration flooding the universe — a cosmic chord sweeping through all of reality — and discovered that tuning their subtle senses to its frequency effected remarkable changes within their being.

The yogis would smile at our search for the missing energy and say it is simply spanda — the dynamic leaping into being of the underlying field of being. They would say that the creative process of becoming is happening all the time and that refined consciousness can participate in this unfolding directly, perceiving it as an internal experience. Reality for them consisted of two basic components: an all-pervasive background field out of which creation emerges and an active or dynamic component that animates the universe. To search for missing energy with our gross senses, then, would be to doom ourselves to failure, since the energy we are looking for is to be found at the vital exchange point where consciousness becomes form. Perhaps we will find a way to access this fluctuating quantum field of creation and destruction through physical means. A considerable amount of energy is already being devoted to trying to tap zero-point energy through technology. In fact, some of the more conservative scientists complain about people siphoning off valuable research money for such endeavors. But there may be other ways. Bohm spoke of an implicate order that emerges and forms the external world. The yogis speak of spanda and a leaping forth of being from an underlying field. Both cite consciousness as integral to the process. It may very well be that, as scientists set out to find the missing energy of the universe, they will be taken directly to the landscape already mapped by these early explorers.

An experience from my own life may speak to the nature of the doorway between consciousness and form. I was deeply involved with a man as he was dying from brain cancer. Due to pressure from a tumor, he had days when he was largely unresponsive to the outer world, and I went to visit him one day when he had sunk into one of these deeper states. While I was massaging his neck — which he liked me to do to ease his discomfort — I fell into something of his state of consciousness. While I was drifting, I had a remarkably vivid dream.

In the dream he was with me and was pointing to a seething field of energy, which he told me was the physical world. I could see places where the field of energy was rising up, becoming more coherent, and touching the realm of light where we stood. He turned to me and said, "Wherever your actions are motivated by love, this is the result."

When we love we gather the fluctuating energy and vibration of creation and help lift it into pure light. The evolution of a human embryo is a lovely illustration of this principle. Upon fertilization a template of creation is released that then proceeds with nearly unstoppable momentum. From the moment of conception, the matrix of possibility encoded in genetic material slowly manifests through the remarkable processes of cellular differentiation and specialization to produce a fully functioning human being.

The dream is worth considering for the concept implicit in it: intention organizes the field of available energy. Our intentions can help organize our physical energy, mobilize our emotional responses, and give us strength to overcome obstacles. When Thomas Edison was perfecting the first light bulb he went through literally thousands of different filament substances trying to find one that would work. What gave him the spirit and strength to continue to push until something new took form? Deep within his being he had an intimation of the finished product. He simply knew that humans could capture a new form of light.

Somehow the capacity to envision an outcome helps to bring it about. A friend of mine — a college quarterback — described his perfect game. "I was in a zone for that game. I knew before I threw the ball that the pass would be completed. I could see the pass before it happened. All I had to do was let go to the inevitable. The pass was perfected before I let go of the football. I knew, in the instant I intended the motion of my arm, that the result was a foregone conclusion. Everything at the end of the pass was present in the beginning."

When our intentions are such powerful determiners of outcome we need to be careful with what we envision. Is our intention to amass more money? Hoard more goods? Avoid pain? Serve others? Help heal the planet? Whatever we choose ought to truly fit our values and align with that which we most deeply love.

If the physical universe does ride like a ripple on a vast sea of consciousness, why don't we experience the underlying field directly? This is a fundamental question I have wrestled with my whole life. As a child I used to spend a month each summer on the Blue Glacier in Olympic National Park where my father had a research station. I sat for hours, watching the ice falls and listening to the unique music of glacial waters. Pockets of warm air rose up from the forests below laden with the scent of Douglas fir and cedar, and as the air temperature shifted the pitch of the water music would shift, too. For some reason I found this event extraordinary. The vibrancy of life seemed to pour out from the beauty of the world around me, and I would have the most cherished of thoughts. The top of my head would tingle and for several moments I would experience a strange exultation. I was inspired. I believe now that I was being afforded a momentary glimpse of the underlying field of energy that directly supports our world.

Recently I had a dream in which I was talking to a friend whose work in social change is very similar to mine. I was asking him how to balance my energy so that I could deal with the flood of tasks and information appearing at my doorstep. In the dream he looked at me and said, "Use the window opened by your insights to let the underlying field of the universe support you." As I woke from the dream I could see and feel that our insights do, indeed, carry with them a sustaining energy of action.

The new discoveries in cosmology are forcing us to admit to an energetics we do not understand and cannot yet see. The sailors who made their way across uncharted seas found their way by the stars above their heads. Now we are studying those same stars, and the curvatures of space and time become the points of light that guide us. The expansion of the universe creates a geometry of being. From the heart of stars and across the fabric of space creation spews forth the elements of our existence, tracing a hidden map of emergence that positions us in a vast cosmological dance. If we can open the windows of our being to the underlying matrix of creation through our insights, intuitions, and creative actions we will be sustained by the organizing, implicate order of the universe.

Notes

1. See Gale E. Christianson, *Edwin Hubble: Mariner of the Nebulae* (University of Chicago Press, 1996), and Alexander S. Sharov, Igor D. Novikov, authors; and Vitaly Kisin, translator, *Edwin Hubble: The Discoverer of the Big Bang Universe*, (Cambridge University Press, 1993). For information on the Internet, see www.time.com/time/time100/ scientist/profile/hubble.html .

2. See Ivars Peterson, *"Circles in the Sky: Detecting the Shape of the Universe,"* (Science News Online, http://www.sciencenews.org/sn_arc98/2_21_98/ bob1/htm). See also Jean-Pierre Luminet, Glenn D. Starkman, and Jeffrey R. Weeks, *"Is Space Finite?"* http://www.scientificamerican.com/ 1999/0499issue/0499weeks.html

3. See J. N. Bahcall and S. T. Weinberg, eds. *Dark Matter in the Universe,* (Jerusalem Winter School for Theoretical Physics, 1986/7). For information on the Internet see James Glanz, "Radiation Ripples from Big Bang Illuminate Geometry of Universe," http://www.nytimes.com/library/ national/science112699sci-big-bang.htm; and Adrienne Robbins, "A History of the Shape of the Universe," http://merlin.alfred.edu/~ast300/ papers/robbins/index.html.

4. See S. K. Lamoreaux, "Demonstration of the Casimir Force in the 0.6 to 6 μM Range," *Physical Review Letters* Vol. 78, no. 1, 6 January 1997: 5 – 8. See also V. M. Mostepanenko and N. N. Trunov, *The Casimir Effect and Its Applications,* (Oxford, 1997); and Larry Spruch, "Long-range (Casimir) Interactions," *Science* 272, 7 June 1996: 1452 – 1455. For information on the Internet, see http://cfawww.harvard.edu/~/ babb/casimir-bib.html .

5. See Heinz R. Pagels, *The Cosmic Code: Quantum Physics as the Language of Nature,* (Bantam Books, 1984).

6. Gambling, which is ubiquitous across cultures, could be an innate human response to a closed and predictable universe that is framed, all too often, by habits and patterns that ossify experience. It may well be that one of the underlying attractions of gambling is that humans get to interact with the probability inherent in the structure of the universe. By relying on the element of chance in the external environment, one is relieved of the stress of inner transformation.

7. There is an amusing story told about Einstein in this regard. One day he went to take a bath; several hours passed and he had not emerged. His step-daughter was concerned and knocked tentatively at the door, asking him if he was all right. When she entered she found him in the tub. He excused himself, explaining that he thought he had been sitting at his desk. He had been busy riding the waves of pure thought and had lost track of his discrete location as an object.

8. See Georg Feuerstein, "The Sacred Syllable OM,"
http://www.yrec.org/om.html.

Additional Resources

INTERNET LINKS

http://darc.obspm.fr/~luminet/etopo.html
An excellent article with great illustrations on the topology of the universe, by Jean-Pierre Luminet; Research Director at CNRS, Astrophysicist at the Paris-Meudon Observatory.

http://donald.phast.umass.edu/~linder/sca.html
Scalar Fields, Quintessence, and the Cosmological Constant.

http://www.jerrypournelle.com/reports/special/negrav.html
A good overview of Quintessence, Dark matter, and the Cosmological Constant.

http://www.lbl.gov/Science-Articles/Archive/dark-energy.html
Dark energy fills the Cosmos. A good article on Quintessence and Dark matter from the Berkeley Laboratory.

BOOKS

Chown, Marcus. *Afterglow of Creation: From the Fireball to the Discovery of Cosmic Ripples.* University Science Books, 1996. ISBN 0935702407

Combs, Allan and Herbert V. Guenther (Introduction). *The Radiance of Being: Complexity, Chaos and the Evolution of Consciousness.* Paragon House, 1997. ISBN 1557787557

Elgin, Duane. *Awakening Earth: Exploring the Evolution of Human Culture and Consciousness.* Millennium Project, 1993. ISBN 0688116213

Hawking, Stephen. *A Brief History of Time.* Bantam Doubleday Dell, 1998. ISBN 0-55310-953-7

Lightman, Alan P. *Ancient Light: Our Changing View of the Universe.* Harvard University Press, 1993. ISBN 0674033639

Livio, Mario. *The Accelerating Universe: Infinite Expansion, the Cosmological Constant, and the Beauty of the Cosmos.* John Wiley & Sons, 2000. ISBN 047132969X

Rowan-Robinson, Michael. *Ripples in the Cosmos: A View Behind the Scenes of the New Cosmology.* Oxford University Press, 1993. ISBN 0716745038

Smolin, Lee. *The Life of the Cosmos.* Oxford University Press, 1999. ISBN 019512664

A WHEEL FOR THE TURNING

Jane Adams was born in the midst of discord as a nation went to war with itself. Her mother died when Jane was two; her father, a Quaker, raised her to have a strong sense of moral purpose and commitment to social causes. She helped alleviate the misery born of poverty that followed the Civil War as industrialization turned rivers of immigrants into fodder for the factories. Hull House (which she founded) offered education, art, and support to the underprivileged of Chicago; and Frank Lloyd Wright, Clarence Darrow, John Dewey, and other contemporary intellectuals visited Hull House to witness her philosophy of caring put into action.

Adams broke the stereotype of women of her time, and her experiment in social service would help shift the conditions of the poor throughout the world. She was instrumental in helping achieve voting rights for women and worked tirelessly in the cause of peace (for which she was awarded a Nobel peace prize). Jane Adams is a clear example of a person whose moral leadership and personal strength effected worthwhile cultural change.

I remember the day she shared the dream with me. A wagon had pulled up outside Hull House and I was helping her unload some provisions for the kindergarten that had started up inside. She paused as she reached to pick up a package from the back of the wagon and stood staring at one of the wheels.

"Isn't this curious," she said. "This reminds me of my dream. A nightmare that that would come over and over again when I was a child." She wrestled the package from its cradle and continued to talk as we walked toward the house. It was just like her not to let a personal reflection interrupt the flow of work.

"I used to dream that all the people in the entire world had died or gone away. I was the only one left. And I knew that unless I could build a wagon wheel, life would not start again. The weight of the world rested on my shoulders. In the dream I would search out a blacksmith's shop and, through my labors, try and build a wheel."

We entered the house as she finished speaking. There were people everywhere. Residents streaming in from their work day. Volunteers appearing to help with classes. Streams of humanity were pouring into the house, and she was the hub to which all the spokes were connected. Her dream suddenly made sense to me. Here in the heart of Chicago, amongst the poorest of immigrants, she had begun to turn a wheel against the forces of oppression. Her compelling intelligence and dedication to a life of action had set the wheel in motion.

I have to laugh when I think back on the discussions we had in Hull House. She was always one to encourage a questing mind — a seeking after of what is true. And the discussions were not tame. Socialists held forth long into the night about ways to bring about the revolution they so hungered for. The frustration of their blocked ambitions generated enough heat to warm even the coldest Chicago night. I have to laugh because, in retrospect, she did more than any of them to change the world. The monopolies didn't lose their strength, but people began to see the need to enforce decent working conditions and to tend to the interests of the powerless and disenfranchised.

And she? She always tended those who were in need. And she tended from a position of such uprightness that whom ever she helped felt ennobled. Condescension and false piety were foreign to her.

"How is it that you can give your care so selflessly?" I asked her once. " It never seems to weaken those around you. Some people I've seen who try to help the poor seem to create more of a burden." We were cleaning up after a birthday party for one of the residents. Most in the house were asleep and she and I were the only ones left. I begged her to sleep, for she was tired and run down — a plea that was justified, in my mind, since she caught typhoid fever a short while later and nearly died.

She paused, as if I had asked a question that had not occurred to her before. She turned to me and said with that no-nonsense look of hers, "I struggled for years to understand what it was I should be doing in this world. And in the end it took my back to show me. After my back operation I was forced to listen — and so I did. I spent two years listening. On my trip to Europe instead of resting, as my doctor would have had me do, I ventured into the poorest of the cities and I listened. When you hear the voice of the world, no matter how that voice comes, you must act."

I assumed the conversation would end there, for it was her way to move briskly on to the next item. But she confounded me as she often has. "You know, one other memory comes. When I was a girl there was a family who lost all but one of its sons in the Civil War. The remaining son was out hunting and was killed in an accident. Our whole town was stunned. How could a family who had lost so much lose yet again? As I, in my young way, tried to grapple with this seeming injustice, it came to me that the answer would only come if I took a large enough view. It was one of my first glimpses into knowing that the resolution to personal problems lies in leaving the small self behind. And that is what I suggest we do this very moment."

And that was that. It was clear as we cleaned the last table that there would be no more discussion. She had heard the call, and it was up to those around her to find a way to listen. She was willing to educate, but she was not willing to indulge. This was her backbone and it brought the most obstinate to their knees. From the days of her childhood she knew she had a job to do here and that is what she did. She set about with her courage, morality, and intelligence to make sure that democracy was more than a name.

I will always think of her as having backbone. This woman, who could not stand entirely straight, stood straighter than anyone I have ever met.

Chapter Nine

TRACING THE WORLD ON YOUR HAND:
A BRIEF TOUR OF PERCEPTION

NIKOLA TESLA WAS DROWNING. He had swum under a large floating platform and become disoriented. In the confusion of shadows, water, and fear he was unable to find a way out, until in the midst of his panic a flash of light showed him a picture of the obstacle, and where he could find a small pocket of air. Guided by his vision he found the air pocket, where he re-oriented himself enough to swim out from under the structure and make it to shore. Tesla's flash of light was not new to him. He had been experiencing similar flashes since he was a small child, and they were often followed by scenes so vivid that he sometimes had trouble distinguishing them from the reality others saw. Once he learned to control the process, Tesla began to observe it more closely. He was to discover that at night he would see images of distant lands and peoples, and he credited these visions with much importance in the later development of his power as an inventor. Tesla says:

> I had noted that the appearance of images was always preceded by an actual vision of scenes under peculiar and generally very exceptional conditions, and I was impelled on

each occasion to locate the original impulse. After a while this effort grew to be almost automatic and I gained great facility in connecting cause and effect. Soon I became aware, to my surprise, that every thought I conceived was suggested by an external impression. Not only this but all my actions were prompted in a similar way. In the course of time, it became perfectly evident to me that I was merely an automaton endowed with the power of movement responding to the stimuli of the sense organs and thinking and acting accordingly.[1]

In 1577 a woman was riding in a coach across the wintry roads of northern Spain. Stopping at a remote inn she discovered, to her surprise, that some old friends were also staying there. In a reverie of warmth a delightful image appeared to her: she saw the image of a castle in which the rooms corresponded to stages on the spiritual journey. St. Teresa of Avila had just seen her way into a creative synthesis of her life's work. This image was to become the foundation of one of the most enduring books in the Christian contemplative tradition — *The Interior Castle*.

Tesla investigated his perceptions and realized that internal phenomena had external causes. St. Teresa of Avila had an organizing map of her life appear before her inner eye. Half a world away, a contemporary of Tesla's was exploring the same issue. As a child, Sri Aurobindo had been sent to England for his education. His father, who died while Aurobindo was still young, was adamant about shielding his son from the superstitions of India and directed that he be kept away from any form of Indian religion. (When Aurobindo returned to India, he had to learn to speak his native language.) Upon his return Aurobindo threw himself into the political arena, working tirelessly toward independence for India. He was very suspicious of yoga, saying he had little use for it. As a consequence it was many years before Aurobindo met his first true yogi — Bhaskar Lele — who agreed to spend three days with him.

Lele gave Aurobindo a single command, "Sit in meditation, but do not think. Look only at your mind. You will see thoughts coming into it. Before they can enter, throw these away from your mind till your mind is capable of entire silence."[2]

Aurobindo took Lele at his word and over the three days entered a state of consciousness in which his mind became as "silent as a windless air on a high mountain." Following this experience Aurobindo gradually withdrew from his political activities and entered a period of intense writing and contemplation, his life forever changed by the experience of grounding his identity in a place beyond thought.

Both Tesla and Aurobindo speak to a fundamental aspect of perception: our thoughts spring from impulses that originate beyond our immediate selves. Aurobindo recorded his amazement at this idea. He said, "I had never before heard of thoughts coming visibly into the mind from outside, but I did not think either of questioning the truth or the possibility, I simply sat down and did it." Where do our perceptions come from, then, if not from ourselves? They arise from introjects — our internalizations of familial and cultural patterns. They come from the gestalt of our world and from the interconnected web of life and being in which we are all embedded. And at some level it seems likely that the universe and everything in it is in constant communication.

In 1926, at roughly at the same time Hubble was discovering that we live in an expanding universe, an Austrian physicist named Erwin Schrodinger made the theoretical prediction that photons can become entangled in such a way that the quantum state of one is instantaneously known by its twin. Even if these photons fly apart a measurement on one will instantaneously alter its counterpart.

Evidence from a Swiss experiment supports Schrodinger's prediction.[3] An impulse of light was split and sent in two directions over two fiber-optic cables, and the signal was tested when the light pulses were seven miles apart. Experimenters discovered that if the phase of one photon was changed, the other instantaneously registered this change — experimental proof of quantum connectivity. Describing the experiment, physicists said that it raises the unsettling possibility that quantum events in the farthest reaches of the universe may influence events here on Earth.

Our perceptions may be part of a reciprocating form of communication similar to that of quanta (and influenced by the same forces). Our physical boundaries are porous, part of the field of interconnecting relationships that make up the universe. Our perceptions perform a fluid dance — cascading, swirling, interacting, and co-creating the world we experience. Perceptions unfold the world and makes it known to our senses. We organize their patterns of input into meaning and derive information about reality from them about reality.

A lovely story from Helen Keller's autobiography speaks to the process of perception. Blind and deaf after contracting a severe fever as a baby, Keller refused to concede to her limitations. The following quote describes how, with the help of teacher Anne Sullivan, Keller first became aware of language.

> We walked down the path to the well-house, attracted by the fragrance of the honeysuckle with which it was covered. Someone was drawing water and my teacher placed my hand under the spout. As the cool stream gushed over one hand, she spelled into the other the word 'water', first slowly, then rapidly. I stood still, my whole attention fixed upon the motions of her fingers. Suddenly I felt a misty consciousness as of something forgotten — a thrill of returning thought; and somehow the mystery of language was revealed to me. I knew that 'w-a-t-e-r' meant the wonderful cool something that was flowing over my hand. That living word awakened my soul, gave it light, hope, joy, set it free! There were barriers still, it is true, but barriers that could in time be swept away.[4]

In pictures of Helen Keller with her teacher, Anne Sullivan, you can see evidence of an essential love; the two developed a life-long companionship that was truly spiritual. It was this remarkable relationship that catalyzed Keller's return from isolation to full engagement with the world. Through compassion her spirit was rekindled. As Keller said of the moment she realized there was a word for what she felt love to be: "The beautiful truth burst upon my mind — I felt that there were invisible lines stretched between my spirit and the spirits of others."

What strikes me as fascinating is Keller's "misty consciousness of something forgotten — a thrill of returning thought." It is as if by accessing language for the first time she were encountering an implicate order of reality. Her perception was akin to remembering. Is our perception, when clarified by our soul's intent, a remembering of an implicate order of reality? Do we literally see into other realms of the world when we are looking correctly? The yogi philosophers of India would certainly hold this view; they say our interior worlds are conditioned by language, formed by letters, and that those letters support external reality. Greek philosophers would agree; they conceived of Logos (from which the words "ecology," "dialogue," and "logic" all derive) as the power of emanation which connects the world we experience to the unknowable creative power of the universe. And Christians the world over believe that, "In the beginning was the Word and the Word became flesh."

The universe, it seems, is constantly talking to us. In Chapter Seven we saw how chaos deconstructs and reconstructs reality. And in Chapter Eight we saw that the material world most likely emerges from an underlying and organized field. In this chapter, and in the first chapter of the book, we have seen how Nikola Tesla, Sri Aurobindo, Helen Keller, and Nainoa Thompson all discovered levels of perception previously unknown to them. In each case that new level of perception led to a greater awareness and clarity. When external structures fail we are afforded the opportunity to learn to see, hear, and feel in new ways. If we do not resist, we begin to find the greater order in events and often discover novel solutions to our dilemmas that could not otherwise have occurred to us.

It is quite common for events to emerge in the world that have their source in levels beyond the reach of daily perceptions; these processes can organize external events in surprising and unpredictable ways. Prior to getting pregnant, a friend of mine suddenly — and with considerable intensity — announced to her partner that they needed to move from shared accommodations to an apartment of their own. During the move, six vehicles experienced some kind of mechanical breakdown. It became something of a joke, and those who knew my friend all commented that something big must have been changing in her life for so much chaos to appear in her environment. Shortly after the move she discovered she was pregnant. The impending arrival of a baby had somehow compelled her to move, and the shift in the structure of her life was accompanied by the mysterious string of vehicular breakdowns. The physical world anticipates and registers changes that emerge from deep within our psyches. During times of increased change or transformation, accidents, weird occurrences, and strange coincidences often seem to appear as if from thin air.

The capacity to see and solve problems within a larger context is essential if we are to survive the challenges that face us. Westerners have a tendency to want to fix problems without necessarily understanding the deeper implications of the fix: we invent DDT to control insect infestations, but end up decimating bird populations and poisoning the land. The end result of our efforts is negative, creating more of a disturbance to the web of life than an enhancement. But it need not be so.

The very act of considering whole systems may change the way our neurology works. As our brain functions change, our perceptions change. As our perceptions change, our ability to see the world changes. In 1962, Rachel Carson released *Silent Spring* and launched a revolution that revitalized an environmental movement eclipsed by postwar attitudes of progress.[5]

Carson's book and actions led to the creation of the Environmental Protection Agency, who began the cleanup of the nation's lands and waters. And her task was not easy. Nearly half a billion dollars' worth of pesticides was sold the year her book came out, and she came under fierce attack from the vested interests of her day.

Rachel Carson's powers of observation made her a good scientist, a fine writer, and a potent agent of change, but it was her vision that moved presidents, members of Congress, and the people of the world to action. We may not all have the destiny of a Rachel Carson, but each of us can help our planet by undertaking the work of seeing clearly. If we attempt to see with our hearts and with our whole selves, the results will be world-changing.

For those who think that changes in perception have little real-world effect, consider the story of Mohammed. In the seventh century this humble man, who had been staring at the stars from a mountaintop in the desert night, began to hear the voice of a greater whole. Over the next few decades he would give voice to the wisdom of his culture, his landscape, and his God. The vision revealed to him welded together a handful of fiercely independent and proud desert warriors into a civilization that was to produce breakthroughs in medicine, science, mathematics, art, architecture, technology, and literature that live on and inform our modern experience.

The task of freeing perception is perennial. Consider this lesson from the Koran, keeping in mind that in Arabic the word "heart" means both "seat of intelligence, understanding, and discrimination" and "seat of emotions, love, and relationship:"

> Do they not travel through the land,
> so that their hearts and minds
> may learn wisdom
> and their ears may learn to hear?
> Truly it is not their eyes which are blind,
> but their hearts which are in their breasts.
> (Sura 22:46)

If our hearts are closed to the pain and suffering of the world, we literally will not be able to see it. And our blindness will lead us to more of the same actions that have pushed our planet toward breakdown. Crises occur when we are out of step with the greater flow of reality. Fear, doubt, and anger freeze us, and we lose our ability to see our way. We fall back into dysfunctional behavior. A similar phenomenon occurs on a more global scale when the perceptions of one collective of people clash with the perceptions of another, creating conflict or outright war.

If everything in the universe is interconnected, it is not much of a stretch to postulate that the physical world registers changes that take place within us. When our perceptions are grounded in fear and small-heartedness we guarantee that the changes that appear will be violent, wrenching, and difficult. Depression, doubt, and fear may emerge from the wounded landscape in which we live, but the wounded landscape also emerges from the traumas that live within us. Self-esteem, our sense of personal identity, and our hopes may, in part, emanate from the world around us, but they also go out into the world and make a difference to it. Exalted ideas may emerge from a realm of being that exists far beyond our usual consciousness, but they also circulate through us and reemerge in the physical world.

In the face of difficult external conditions, simple kindness is the medicine that can heal both internally and externally. There was once a group of six men who worked in a nuclear weapons plant. Each one alone in his heart of hearts despised the work he was doing, but each had a family to support and felt trapped by the forces of circumstance. The six formed a support group to grapple with their tensions and to listen to the voices of their hearts. The men made a unique pact. All six would support one man at a time as he left the plant to look for different work. One by one each man made the break, supported all the while by their net of friendship and mutual kindness.

The future is not fixed. Fate is not determined, except by our lack of willingness to cleanse the doorways of our perception and see. When we commit to seeing truth, the challenges we face — though difficult — have within them the seeds of higher function.

Notes

1. This excerpt appeared in a short biographical sketch, *The Strange Life of Nikola Tesla*, transcribed and released by John Roland Penner; no copyright. Used with permission.   Jpenner@Genie.GEIS.com

2. See Satprem, *Sri Aurobindo or the Adventure of Consciousness* (Institute for Evolutionary Research, 1993), p. 41 for the three quotations referring to Sri Aurobindo's meditation experience.

3. See Malcolm W. Browne, "Signal Travels Farther and Faster Than Light," http://pages.nyu.edu/~yqv7599/sci-quan.htm .

4. See Helen Keller, *The Story of My Life* (Buccaneer Books, 1976), pp. 36 and 41 for the quotations referring to Helen Keller's experience of language and her recognition of connection to others.   Used with permission.

5. See http://RachelCarson.org for material on Rachel Carson and her work.

Additional Resources

INTERNET LINKS

http://www.tesla.org/
An overview of Nikola Tesla and his work.

http://www.xdk96dial.pipex.com/tesla.html
A good brief biography of Nikola Tesla.

http://www.highvoltage.8m.com/frameset.htm?autobio.htm
An extensive Tesla site, including his autobiography.

http://www.sriaurobindosociety.org.in/index.htm
Web site of the Sri Aurobindo Society.

http://sriaurobindoinstitute.org/sriauro.html
Sri Aurobindo Institute of Culture.

http://www.miraura.org/home.html
The Integral Yoga of Sri Aurobindo. Extensive biographies are available at this site.

http://tlc.ai.org/keller.htm
Resources for studying Helen Keller.

http://www.afb.org/afb.org/afb/archives/intro.html
  The Helen Keller Archival Collection.

http://www.rachelcarson.org/
  The Rachel Carson Homestead Association. A good source for material on her.

Books

Books by and about Sri Aurobindo:

Aurobindo, Sri. *Savitri: A Legend and a Symbol*. Auromere, 1940. ISBN 0897449347

Aurobindo, Sri, author; and M. P. Pandit, compiler. *Gems From Sri Aurobindo*. Lotus Press, 1991. ISBN 0941524337

Ghose, Aurobindo and Sri Aurobindo. *The Integral Yoga: Sri Aurobindo's Teaching and Method of Practice*. Lotus Press, 1998. ISBN 0941524760

Satprem, Sri *Aurobindo or The Adventure of Consciousness*. Institute for Evolutionary Research, 1993. ISBN 0938710044

Books by and about Rachel Carson:

Lear, Linda J. *Rachel Carson: Witness for Nature*. Owl Books, 1998. ISBN 0805034285

Carson, Rachel. *Silent Spring*. Houghton Mifflin, 1994. ISBN 0395683297

Books by and about Helen Keller:

Helen and Teacher: The Story of Helen Keller and Anne Sullivan Macy. Radcliffe Biography Series. Perseus Press, 1997. ISBN 0201694689

Keller, Helen. *Story of My Life*. Doubleday, 1991. ISBN 0553213873

Books by and about Nikola Tesla:

Johnston, Ben, ed. *My Inventions: The Autobiography of Nikola Tesla*. Hart Brothers, 1982. ISBN 0910077002

O'Neil, John Jacob. *Prodigal Genius: The Life of Nikola Tesla*. Angriff Press, 1944. ISBN 0913022403

Wise, Tad. *Tesla: A Biographical Novel of the World's Greatest Inventor*. Turner, 1994. ISBN 1570361630

Interlude

WHEN THE RAINS CAME

*Black Elk was a Lakota Sioux holy man born previous
to contact with whites. If ever a man had to negotiate difficult
tides of change and still hold the spiritual depth of his people,
it was Black Elk: he lived to see his people decimated, the buffalo
killed off, and the prairie tamed. He felt he failed to enact the
great vision given to him as a nine-year-old boy when, over a
period of a week as he lay as one dead, he was shown a
magnificent vision of the spiritual renewal of mankind.
This Interlude chronicles a real journey that Black Elk made up
Mount Harney near the end of his life, and its outcome is true.*

It was hot and dusty when we set off up the mountain, and
the wind was coming from every direction, unable to make
up its mind. "A seven-direction wind," he whispered to me.
"It comes from all corners." I wasn't so sure. It seemed annoying and not holy. But then, I have often found that the truly
sacred can be the most annoying, so who am I to say?

He said that if the spirits were happy with his life perhaps
some rain would come. I looked at the dusty prairie below us
and the blue sky around us and secretly prayed that my friend
would be spared another disappointment.

When I heard he wanted to go to the top of Harney Peak and pray one last time, I had felt a stirring in the dried-up springs of my hope. When you hunger for rain, you begin to feel the want in your bones. And the earth had been thirsty for weeks. The maker of clouds had abandoned the prairie and badlands, and day after day the blue sky pressed down against the earth. The tender shoots of grass that feed the green lands had all turned brown. When I pulled a clump from the ground they hung dead in my grasp.

Not only the land had withered — something in the dry wind depressed the spirit. Sadness kept me from rising before the morning star. True, our people had survived and renewed a sense of our destiny. But fewer and fewer of us held to the old ceremonies, and the flood of strange ways threatened to wash our young from their roots. Even I could see less and less of the Great Mystery in what was around me. Surviving had taken the wind from the soaring of the hawk.

When we were young Black Elk and I would wake before the rest of the camp, sneak through the single door of the tipi, and race to the creek to watch for the reflection of the morning star. He said once, "If you see the star's reflection, then the spirits will know that you are humble. If you do not look too quickly to the source you may understand what the

Great Mystery wants of you." Only after we saw the star in the water below would we dare look up and see it in the bright sky of morning. And then we would dive into the waters, screaming as the cold washed the night away and brought us into day. But we are old now, and he has been looking too long, I think, into the other world. He has mist across his eyes and is almost blind. And I find that the sounds of the world have faded. I must strain to hear the speech of my friends, and even the hawk's call is muffled. So we hiked slowly that day, stopping often to rest.

When we reached the top of the mountain he brought out his pipe and unwrapped it — all of his movements slow and deliberate. The stem was as weathered as his hands. Oil and countless prayers had soaked into the wood — memories of all the moments he has spent with this precious companion. I am afraid I did not hear the words of his prayer. My weakened ears could not bring the sound of his voice into my heart. But he was pleading for forgiveness for failing to bring forth his vision, given so long ago. This, I know, was the kernel of his prayer.

I saw him raise high his pipe, and all the love I have for him, all the memories, all the hopes lost and the ones found, came at once — like a seven-direction wind. This man who had bravely kept the secret of his vision alive, who had danced through the deepest of my people's darkness to keep hope alive, who had struggled always to help us, was asking for forgiveness. So full was my heart and so far away were my thoughts that I failed to notice when clouds came up around us. It wasn't until I felt the first few drops of rain that I returned to myself and looked at my friend.

His eyes, which could see so little now, were spilling out the gratitude in his heart. For the spirits had answered him, and the Thunder Beings were loose once again upon the breast of the Earth. I saw him smile as he heard them speak. It was a smile of relief and of humor — as if he truly understood the joke of us poor two-leggeds ever really understanding the Great Mystery.

The rain fell softly around us and the thunder echoed long across the afternoon.

Listening to the thunder and watching the rain mix with his tears, I knew that he had not failed. He had served his people faithfully and kept the fire of hope alive through our darkness — gift enough to give back to the Maker of all these lands. The Great Mystery is so deep that no one human can fully hold the basket of that power. This humble-hearted man, friend of my youth — and now of my age — had brought back the rain.

"It is good," was all he said to me on that mountaintop. And it was — the coming of the rain, the prayer, my friend's life, this world. It is good.

Chapter Ten

"NEW FIELDS OF LIFE EXPLORING:"
INTUITION AND CULTURE SHIFTS

L ATE ONE AFTERNOON in February of 1882, a tall man and
his friend were taking a walk toward a gorgeous sunset in
Budapest. The light of the sun as it crept toward the darkness of
night bathed the two in an uncommon beauty. Only a short time
before, the man had been bedridden, unable to tolerate the least
disturbance of his senses. The sound of a ticking watch a few rooms
away was unbearable. The vibration of traffic, communicated
through the frame of the house he was in, was so painful that rub-
ber pads had been placed under his body to try and shield him
from the noise. His pulse rate varied dramatically. Even the pressure of sunlight on his body was intolerable. The doctors who
attended him were baffled. But the man was determined to survive
because he knew he was to bring an invention to the world. So he
had held the possibility of this invention close to his heart like a tal-
isman that could guide him through the agony of his illness. Finally
he had recovered and was able to go out once again.

On the streets of Budapest that February day in 1882, the
beauty of the winter sun inspired the man, and he turned to his
friend and quoted a few lines from Goethe's *Faust:*

The glow retreats, done is the day of toil;
It yonder hastens, new fields of life exploring;
Ah, that no wing can lift me from the soil,
Upon its track to follow, follow soaring . . .

Light, poetic inspiration, and the lingering effects of the man's heightened sensitivity suddenly coalesced. Like a great breath drawing inward, his attention gathered into a point of concentration and for a time he was silent.

As his friend wondered what had come over his companion, Nikola Tesla picked up a twig from the ground and sketched a quick diagram of his invention in the dust. It was the only blueprint he ever made.

In the moment of his silence Tesla had seen the solution to a power propagation problem, and the structure for an alternating current generator had suddenly become clear in his mind. (Later, in a machine shop in Paris, Tesla was to mill a perfectly working model of his generator, referring only to the visualization he held in his mind.) Capable of creating a rotating magnetic field, Tesla's invention became the driving mechanism for the modern electrical grid. (When he was 13 Tesla had told his parents that one day he would "light up the world" from Niagara Falls.) With the backing of Westinghouse, the first of several major generators was set up at Niagara Falls, and New York City became a beacon to the world.[1]

Intuition — the faculty of knowing without recourse to rational processes — is our birthright and has been a tool for navigating the changing material universe since the first human hunters appeared. Our hunter-gatherer ancestors needed to know how to find game, so they evolved techniques for reading the patterns of nature that helped them to hunt successfully and survive. And they used oracles (seers, shamans) to predict the outcome of future events. Elaborate rituals for shifting consciousness added information to what their senses could tell them. In other words, they developed a methodology for integrating intuition into their everyday lives.

We need what intuition can teach us. *Kundun,* a film based on the life of the current Dalai Lama, provides us with a dramatic portrayal of the intuitive function.[2] In several sequences we see the Dalai Lama and his counselors consult an Oracle-seer. This man, trained to enter other states of consciousness, falls into a trance and utters predictions which are used to help guide the actions of the young Dalai Lama as he wrestles with guiding the Tibetan people during their brutal invasion by the Chinese.

In our own lives, dreams can provide one valuable way by which we can begin to access a larger field of knowing. The democracy of the dream world is absolute. Everyone dreams. Every night everyone shifts for a time out of normal consciousness to encounter other dimensions of life.

Dreams encode messages about our bodies, emotional lives, relationships and, ultimately, our location in the cosmos. Deaths have been announced in dreams — Lincoln dreamt of his own death. The future can be revealed in dreams — General Schwarzkopf dreamt he was going to be wounded in Vietnam before he actually was. Inventions are made evident in dreams. Solutions to health problems are suggested in dreams. And spiritual guidance appears in dreams.

To access the larger field of knowing we simply need to learn the language of dreams and suspend the cynicism of our waking minds, which judge information from the dream world as less than that reported through our five senses. Dreams speak to us from an expansive realm. They speak in a poet's voice and in symbols. If we choose to listen, we can gain a much-needed ally in the task of navigating the tides of change.

Tell someone your dreams on a regular basis — the act of remembering and reciting them will help strengthen the muscles of the dream body. You do not need dictionaries of symbols nor do you need some esoteric knowledge to unlock your dreams — they are as fundamental as breath to the human experience.

When you make the commitment to value your dreams and begin to share them, it will help open the doorway to understanding their meaning.

A brief map of the dream world may be helpful at this point. Like waking experiences, dream experiences can vary widely, though they can generally be placed in one of three categories:

Dreams induced from physical conditions

Dreams that arise from disturbances in the physical body tend to cycle the same material over and over. With fever dreams, for instance, a looping process occurs and a particular dream sequence is repeated. Physiological stress brought on by overeating can also produce repetitive dreams. Often the dream will encode body symptoms that mirror the physical discomfort. Dreams that emanate from physiological disturbances do not usually have a strong component of meaning associated with them and should be treated as symptoms of physical imbalance.

Dreams that sort our daily lives

By far the most common type of dream, dreams that take material from our daily lives and replay it. Personal issues, emotional concerns, and other daily struggles will appear in the dream state, usually symbolically represented. Decoding the symbols is best done using a simple associative process. By taking each element of your dream and asking what it reminds you of in your waking life, you can begin to decode the message.

Dreams in this category almost always have solutions to personal dilemmas embedded in them. Sometimes the solution is as simple as helping to reframe the problem; at other times the solutions are quite specific. The solutions may not always be immediately apparent, but with consistent effort they will emerge.

Visionary Dreams

Visionary dreams are not as frequent as dreams from the other two categories. In fact, we may only have a handful of these dreams in our lifetime. These dreams are vivid, powerful emissaries from the core of life. Precognition, philosophical insight, visions of life purpose, and information about other people and places can all appear in this level of dreaming. These dreams almost have a luminous quality that lingers long after we have wakened from them. If you have had a visionary dream, there is no doubt in your mind about its impact.

While dreams can act as a conduit to larger realms, we can access those realms in our waking moments too. Lest you think we cannot integrate intuition-based consciousness with real life, I would like to tell you a personal story that shows that we can. When I was a child my father was chief snow ranger at Alta, Utah; he made the decision to open or close ski areas after a winter storm. The lives of thousands of people and the economic interests of the resort all rested on his judgment — a high-stakes judgment call indeed.

I would watch him the morning after a storm. He would consult weather data, checking temperature, wind speed, and snow accumulation totals. Invariably he would step outside and, with a small folding magnifying lens, look at the structure of the snowflakes. And then he would pause, as if waiting for something. A mood would come over him that I could feel even through the double-paned windows that separated me from where he stood in the snow. Then, and only then, would he make his decision.

My father talks openly about the role of intuition in the fine art of avalanche forecasting, and he has written a scientific paper about it. He has also interviewed many of the best avalanche forecasters of his era, nearly all of whom identify intuition as essential to their work. Throughout his career — whether he was overseeing remote research stations or caretaking expeditions into the mountains or onto glaciers — no one ever had a serious injury or accident on my father's watch.

Here's another story about intuition and real life. A friend of mine was in the Northridge earthquake in Southern California. Minutes before the quake hit she woke up to see her spiritual teacher seemingly standing at the foot of her bed. The woman told her to lie very still and she would be fine. Moments later the building began to shake violently. My friend lay quietly in her bed, trusting in her teacher's assurances. When the quake was over she stepped through the chaos of her room and went outside only to hear the sound of sirens gathering from all corners of the dawn. Had she attempted to flee, she most likely would have been injured.

When we incorporate intuition into our lives we assume that we can interact in meaningful ways with modes of reality that exist beyond the obvious domain of our senses. Intuition broadens our view beyond the confines of our merely reasoning minds. We see much more holistically. When the broader web of relationships is experienced first-hand we get better at making good choices.

In periods of intense change — whether personal or collective — intuition is one of our most important tools. We cannot possibly assemble the systems or gather the knowledge required to track all the dimensions of change that are active in our world. We must appeal to a deeper aspect of our human experience and come to trust the knowing of intuition to help guide us unerringly through the maze of external experiences.

It takes courage to listen to the inner prompting of our intuition. How many times have we — or people we know — given up on a dream in order to conform to the spoken or unspoken expectations of families or friends? Sadly, our fear of being expelled from the tribe often blocks us from acting in the way we know is right for us. The wisdom of intuition often runs counter to familiar norms. And that will seem dangerous, radical, and unsettling to those who have an investment in maintaining the status quo.

Examine the lives of the greatest agents of change in this epoch and you will find that easy living was not part of their calling. Gandhi endured fasts, imprisonment, and enmity from his own people, and ultimately an assassin's bullet in order to follow his sense of personal guidance. Until he committed suicide, Alan Turing endured persecution and ridicule over his sexual orientation by the same British government that knighted him for the brilliance of his work with computers. Mother Teresa chose a life of hardship and utter poverty in order to answer the call to service that she heard from within. Each of these innovators suffered, yet came to be celebrated as heroes of our time.

Intuition is not always comfortable nor is it predictable. One of the more maddening things about intuitive wisdom is that we will often get instructions without a timeline or a calendar to go with the information. The following story is one example of an idea that was ahead of its time.

In 1840, Norfolk Island was inarguably the harshest piece of real estate in the British Empire.[3] The island was the final holding ground for the most incorrigible prisoners who had been shipped to Australia in exile. The prison code of the island was severe: floggings, shackling, and starvation were common. In May of that year Alexander Maconochie arrived to take up his new post as commander of the island.

Maconochie ordered that the prison doors be opened and the bewildered prisoners unchained. Then he invited them all to the harbor for a feast. Rum was served, paid for out of pocket by the new commandant. After they had eaten and drunk in sumptuous style, the convicts were treated to an afternoon of drama followed by a fireworks display.

In fact the new commandant initiated a startling new concept in prison management: rehabilitation based on kindness and support. Music therapy was offered; support groups were considered; and the island library was stocked with literature to uplift the men.

A new regimen of gentleness replaced the old horrors. One of the most intractable of prisoners, who had been living more like an animal than a man, was gently introduced to new responsibilities. In a short time he became a devoted attendant to the new commandant. His demeanor and attitude were so changed that visitors to the island who had known him before did not recognize him.

It is a sad but true commentary on human behavior that innovations arising from deep compassion and spiritual wholeness are seldom met with easy acceptance. And so it was with the penal colony on Norfolk Island. Maconochie's ideas were thought too radical, too far ahead of their time. Reactionary forces in the British penal system clamped down and removed the commandant from the island. And after their brief experience with enlightened rehabilitation practices, the prisoners were again treated with the sodden cruelty of the mid-1800s. Were Maconochie's ideas wrong? No, they were not. He was simply ahead of his time.

Each one of us has access to a realm of knowing that can speak directly from the song of the universe. Sustained questioning of any line of inquiry will, over time, yield an intuitive insight into the problem at hand. The key to this inquiry is the application of will and the suspension of disbelief that clouds our capacity to trust in realms beyond our rational understanding. Intuition is not magic. It is not some toy to be used and cast aside without regard for its function or its sacredness. It is a faculty that exists within each of us. Most innovations and inventions — theoretical, social, or technological — have arrived on the wings of insight and intuition, appearing as impulses within some human heart and mind. Our task now is to stretch the limits of our understanding.

Notes

1. This excerpt appeared in a short biographical sketch, *The Strange Life of Nikola Tesla,* transcribed and released by John Roland Penner; no copyright. Used with permission. Jpenner@Genie.GEIS.com. See Tad Wise, *Tesla* (Turner Publishing, 1994) for a fictional treatment of this episode.

2. See *Kundun* [Videotape]. Directed by Martin Scorsese; written by Melissa Mathison. Touchstone Pictures, 1997.

3. See Robert Hughes, *The Fatal Shore* (Vintage Books, 1988).

Additional Resources

INTERNET LINKS

http://www.zades.com.au/suziez/norfolk.html
Norfolk Island history.

http://www.zades.com.au/suziez/norfolk.html
A site filled with information on the Dalai Lama.

BOOKS

Bstan-Dzin-Rgya-Mtsho, Robert B. Livingston, and Zara Houshmand, eds. *Consciousness at the Crossroads: Conversations with the Dalai Lama on Brain Science and Buddhism.* Snow Lion Publications, 1999. ISBN 1559391278

Diamond, Jared. *Guns, Germs, and Steel: The Fates of Human Societies.* W. W. Norton, 1999. ISBN 0393317552

Orloff, Dr. Judith. *Dr. Judith Orloff's Guide to Intuitive Healing: Five Steps to Physical, Emotional, and Sexual Wellness.* Times Books, 2000. ISBN 0812930975

Rogers, Naomi. *Dirt and Disease: Polio Before FDR, Health and Medicine in American Society.* Rutgers University Press, 1992. ISBN 0813517869

Simpkinson, Charles H., author; and Helen Palmer, editor. *Inner Knowing:Consciousness, Creativity, Insight, and Intuition.* J. P. Tarcher, 1999. New Consciousness Reader. ISBN 0874779367

Tesla, Nikola and David Hatcher. *The Fantastic Inventions of Nikola Tesla.* Adventures Unlimited Press, 1993. The Lost Science Series. ISBN 0932813194

The Dalai Lama. *Ethics for the New Millennium.* Riverhead Books, 1999. ISBN 1573220256

—————. *Freedom in Exile: The Autobiography of the Dalai Lama.* Harper San Francisco, 1991. ISBN 0060987014

Vaughan, Frances E. *Awakening Intuition.* Anchor Books/Doubleday, 1979. ISBN 0385133715

A VOICE IN THE GARDEN

Florence Nightingale came from an upper-class British family that held unconventional ideas about the education of daughters: Nightingale was widely read in science, philosophy, mathematics, and other disciplines then considered to be solely within the purview of men. Her interest in alleviating suffering began early, and she would take time to tend servants who had fallen ill and to treat family pets.

Nightingale was clearly able to create a coherent, vital, and life-affirming response to the misery that she saw during her lifetime. She developed the fundamentals of nursing (raising that discipline to a respectable profession) and field-tested them in a hospital in Istanbul where she treated the wounded from the Crimean War. Upon her return to England she shunned fame, and though she spent most of the rest of her long life as an invalid — due to the effects of wartime stress — Nightingale never lost her concern for others. One of the most prolific letter writers in modern times — some twenty thousand letters have been traced to her hand — Nightingale remained a powerful advocate for others in a variety of causes.

She was standing near the bed of a wounded soldier, tallying up a list of hers. It was late, near midnight, and the daytime activities of the hospital had finally subsided as the wave of men who had come in during the waking hours settled for the night. The soldier stirred in pain and she switched her attention from list to man.

Her thin face softened as she raised the soldier's hand from the bed and held it in her own. I watched her trace a gentle path of reassurance over his hand with the same attention to detail that she evidenced in so much of her life. I do not think there was anything about that soldier that escaped her notice in those few moments of contact.

I had been on the other side of that attention many times. And let me tell you, it was not always pleasant. If she saw that you had misplaced an item or that you didn't know where to find something, she would look at you with a fierceness that needed no words.

As I followed her on her rounds I often marveled at how she could hold so many details in her mind and still have room for such a fine heart. Those details! In another life or in another time she might have been a philosopher or a mathematician. But here, at the edge of the Crimea, she was a tireless servant.

Keeping up with her was nearly impossible. She had the energy of seven people, and she cut through the confusion and distress of that hospital with the sheer force of her concentration. She had a childlike love of statistics. "God speaks to us through the numbers," she said. As I watched her with her many lists, I did not doubt that it was true.

She was everywhere and nowhere. And that was the odd thing about her. The closer I got to her, the harder she was to understand. She seemed to have become more than herself. I asked her once how she came by her prodigious energy.

"It was the garden," she responded.

"The garden?" I asked.

"Yes, it was the garden back in England. I was outside one day in my seventeenth year. Early spring green was pushing up through the earth. I was studying the shape of this new life, when suddenly I felt an overwhelming presence."

"Presence?"

"Well, it is difficult to explain. I was simply filled with more than I am. And with the filling came the certainty that I had a distinct mission from God. I was given a job here."

"Did you know then that it would be nursing?"

"No. It took seven more years before that became clear."

"How did you know? How did you know what was the

right path?" Standing next to her was like standing next to a clear, cool waterfall of purpose. I felt so indecisive about my own calling that I pressed the conversation further.

"The path rose around me until I was walking in the direction I was meant to go. This is how it is when we are following our call."

I was filled with envy at that moment. She was so completely certain of herself.

"How can one be called and not another?" I asked. And as I asked, a soldier in a bed near me moaned. She instantly dropped our conversation and turned to the duty at hand. It was like that with her. Her priorities were never selfish. And talking about herself always seemed to make her nervous.

Several days later, she happened to say to me, "All have a calling from life, but not all calling is the same. There is too much variety in this world of ours for any two of us to hear exactly the same voice."

I knew then that she had been thinking about my question. It was just like her to stay with a detail until it had been accounted for. I am not sure I had the answer to my question, but I at least had a sign of her concern for me. And from one such as Florence Nightingale, that was enough.

Chapter Eleven

Frozen Past and Dancing Present:
Our Personal Response to Change

For most of my adult life, I have had to travel a great deal. The closer I get to the time of leaving, the more fragmented my attention becomes, the harder it is to organize what I need to take, and the more tired I become. I often end up exhausted before I ever get on the plane. When I began to explore this phenomenon with more conscious attention, I found myself returning again and again to a story my mother told me about my birth.

My mother's labor had begun and she had gone to the hospital. Once there her contractions stopped, and she was given pitocin (a drug to induce labor). Shortly after the injection her contractions began again in earnest and I was born very quickly. I was placed in the newborn nursery and promptly fell into a deep sleep. In fact, I was so unresponsive that the nurses became concerned about me and spent hours trying to waken me.

The pattern of my adult response to leaving home mirrors the circumstances of my birth. As I ready myself to leave, I anticipate the process and am fairly focused. Then, almost invariably, my forward motion for packing stops and I grow listless and tired. That is followed by a period when I get frantic and disorganized. Finally, after a burst of energy and effort, I experience a profound tiredness.

I have little doubt that I have been re-creating my birth experience as I respond to change in my environment. I have grown better at managing the feelings and anticipating my responses, but many of the cues still exist within me.

Our life story profoundly conditions how we adapt to change. As we saw with the preceding example, birth can leave a dramatic imprint, determining how we respond to change even as adults. But birth is not the only transition that leaves an imprint. We keep indelible records of our previous adaptations and patterns of response encoded in our tissue, layered in our bodies, and stored as deep memory in our minds.

As a child I spent time every summer in the high mountains at my father's research station. I remember one summer making the discovery that the ice in the glacier was hundreds of years old. I remember thinking that I was looking at time slowly moving across the mountain. Talk to any good massage therapist and they will tell you that the past can be, and often is, frozen in our bodies. Bodywork on the knees may bring out memories of terror from childhood. Work on the stomach may trigger rage at being abused at some point in the past. Work on the face may rouse memories of old shame. Unless we review our self-limiting patterns, we remain frozen in the past and are unable to live and respond fully in the present moment.

In some ways our physical bodies — and our awareness — are glacial in their processes. Fields of frozen sensation, function, and awareness exist and move slowly through the landscape of our lives. Every once in a while, some of the glacier melts and we are filled with waterfalls of possibilities. I believe we are called to free ourselves from the glaciers within and regain the energy, vitality, and creative capacity that is our birthright. We have an immense potential to experience and express the dance of the universe within our own bodies and minds (there are more possible connections between neurons in the brain than there are stars), but how do we go about liberating it?

Attention is the golden fire that can free our frozen energy, and we can cultivate it in a variety of ways. Attention comes from a Latin word, meaning "to turn one's mind." By the simple act of turning our minds toward the depth of our own experience, we can begin a process of release that is life-changing. Spiritual practices and disciplines, for instance, begin with work at the level of simple attention; while the focuses of concentration prescribed may vary, attention itself is fundamental. And the actual execution of the practice is far more difficult than it sounds at first blush. The mind is unruly. Quite soon everything but the task at hand will fill the consciousness. Tiredness, lethargy, dullness, random thoughts, old memories, fears, angers, resentments, and a host of other sensations may appear. The steady practice of witnessing our body/mind sensations, however, begins the process of freeing trapped energy, helping us to penetrate cosmic structures and unravel the mysteries of life in a direct and measured manner.

Just as attention moves energy and matter in the outer environment, so it moves energy in our inner environment — with sometimes even more powerful consequences. When we pay attention to the inner world our focus can slowly dissolve the contractions in our bodies and mind that limit our responsiveness to change. Focus comes from the Latin word for "a place of fire." When we let our attention rest upon our body/mind, the warmth of its fire helps us to relax some of the frozen or numbed parts of our bodies.

Mindfulness — the capacity to witness the totality of one's body and mind with equanimity — not only frees frozen energy but leads us to compassion and steadiness of purpose in our relationship to the rest of the world. Thich Nhat Hanh, the Vietnamese Buddhist monk who witnessed firsthand the near-genocide of his people and the ravaging of his homeland during years of war, has led numerous retreats for Vietnam veterans in America to help them come to terms with their wartime experiences. (More Vietnam vets have committed suicide than were killed in the war — a measure of the level of suffering being addressed.) Thich Nhat Hanh's compassion toward the very men who were the killers and destroyers is a testimony to the depth of his spiritual practice of mindfulness.

Spiritual practice is not the only way we can cultivate attention. It is important that we have witnesses to our lives. We can consult trained counselors and therapists, whose capacity to listen without judging can teach us how to pay attention to our stories. Those stories need to be told if we are to free ourselves from the ice of our silences or our fears. We can also seek out soul friends — people we know who can really listen with both heart and mind. Witnessing is a high and generous gift we give each other — a declaration of solidarity and support.

Caring for our bodies is another way that we can cultivate attention. Movement, breath, proper nutrition, sound, and the proper use of concentration can release stress and rebalance our body responses. Exercise (or movement of the body) aids a host of processes from digestion to kidney function. And it balances nervous system functioning. Sensory input that is not counterbalanced by physical activity overloads the system, making us jumpy, irritable, and self-absorbed. Exercise keeps our bodies physically healthy and releases the endorphins that elevate our moods and reinforce our sense of general well-being.

Breath is crucial for life. Physical respiration goes on as a largely unconscious process as the body exchanges oxygen and carbon dioxide to power the activities of every cell in our bodies. Deliberate deep breathing will ensure that we take in enough oxygen and can calm feelings of breathlessness or panic. But we can cultivate respiration in other ways, too. Conscious breathing used during labor and childbirth, as part of a spiritual practice, or as a simple calming technique, focuses the mind's attention and helps relieve stress on our bodies.

Proper nutrition builds and sustains health. Unfortunately, in the West our physical need for food and our eating habits have become unhealthily entwined with psychological, sexual, and cultural imperatives, and eating disorders abound. It can be difficult to change our food choices and eating patterns. As we explore our eating habits, however, we can learn to prepare food that truly nourishes us. And we can learn to make eating a service, an act that can help us re-establish a healthy relationship with food.

Sound purifies the body, aligns the molecular activity of the internal organs, and releases stress that cannot be released in any other way.[1] It elevates the emotions and helps give depth to our daily experiences. I am not talking here about noise pollution but rather those sounds that are deeply organized and that give pleasure — music, chanting, toning, and the sounds of nature, for instance. (This kind of sound can heal. Benedictine monks in France who gave up their daily chanting soon fell ill with colds and flu. Their health was restored when they reinstated chanting as part of their daily routines.) From the Aborigines in Australia who say the Creator sang the world into being, to the ancient Egyptians who believed that the singing sun woke the Earth each day with its cry of light, to the mystics in India who believe that *Nada Bhrama* (the sound of the Creator) forms the substrate of all existence, sound is linked the world over to sacredness. By joining with sound we join in the song of the cosmos.

Proper use of concentration builds a subtle bridge between the structures of our tissues and the movement of our wills. As body-centered disciplines such as martial arts and yoga have demonstrated, there is a profound link between a concentrated mind and the flow of energy in the body: physical stamina, strength, and elegance of movement are its hallmarks. Proper use of concentration rebalances pathways of communication within the body that are easily interrupted by stress or neglect. As the easy flow of energy from the mind to the body and from the body to the mind is restored, stress is reduced and we gain new confidence in our bodies.

When we pay attention — whether we use spiritual, psychological, or physical means (or a combination of them) — we change our relationship with the world. As we give credence to ourselves and allow all information about our experience to surface, our focus broadens, and we slowly dissolve the contractions of body and mind which limit our responsiveness to life and its ever-changing patterns. Ultimately, when we pay attention our vision clears and we stabilize ourselves in the present. But that is not the end of the story.

Our personal history is not the only history we embody; we need to understand our biological history, as well, if we are to learn to respond to the times in useful ways. As we develop in the womb we recapitulate the dance of evolution, marking our membership in the pageant of life that has unfolded through time. The structure of our brains is one of the many legacies of that evolutionary dance. Brain research in the last few decades has advanced credible and conclusive evidence that when we are faced with change our responses are conditioned by four distinct brain structures — each with its own needs, responses, and adaptive styles.

The reptilian brain is the oldest part of the brain and is found at its core. This part of the brain is concerned with issues of survival, power, and display; rituals and ceremonies of any kind appeal to it since they help give structure to powerful urges and desires that course through it.

Curved around the reptilian brain is a structure called the limbic system. This structure is considered an outgrowth and adaptation of the mammalian brain, and its concerns are primarily emotional and social. Our need to belong, our desire to be part of a small group, and our sense of social identity have their ground in the limbic center.

Situated over the limbic center is a structure known as the neocortex. This part of the brain is concerned with language and abstractions, and will function with little attention to or concern about feelings and bodily sensations. Symbols, mathematics, and the structure of language appeal to this part of the brain.

Finally, at the front of the brain we find the frontal lobes — a specialized adaptation of the neocortex. This area of the brain is concerned with pattern recognition. Therefore, our ability to recognize that deep structures organize the field of world events is a function of this area of the brain. Interestingly, the frontal lobes have also been linked to self-talk, that continuous internal conversation we have with ourselves that maintains our sense of self and identity. The frontal lobes also house our capacity for altruism and self-sacrifice.

How we adapt to sudden change is deeply influenced by the part of the brain from which we respond. If we are used to responding from our reptilian brain — the one that codes events as a survival issue — then change could trigger a 'me-first' or even a violent response. People who hoard or steal food when they think there may be a shortage are making a response from their reptilian brain.

If we are accustomed to respond from the limbic center, then outer change will intensify our desire to belong, to be a part of something greater. The rapid growth of Hitler youth groups in post World War I Germany is a good example of people whose limbic-centered responses were based on emotion that took the form of fierce loyalty and patriotism.

If we primarily access the world through the functions of the neocortex, then ideas, symbols, and abstractions become the filters by which we navigate change. Einstein's formulation of his theory of relativity in the midst of the chaotic changes brought about by World War I is a good example of this kind of response.

Finally, if we tend to respond to change from our frontal lobes, then we will look for the larger patterns at work in any local circumstances and will most probably have the capacity to respond altruistically. Gandhi is a great example of someone with a highly developed frontal lobe capacity. He was able to discern patterns of behavior in political processes that gave him an uncanny ability to pick the right timing and action for the most effective outcome — and his actions benefited millions.

There seems to be a relationship between frontal lobe capacity and selflessness. It has been my observation that when people begin to consider the larger patterns of events, when they begin to ask big-picture questions, when they begin to think globally, their self-talk can sometimes diminish. The patterns of the whole, the subtlety of the greater dance of life, and the recognition of the inherent elegance of that dance quiets their constant need to reference a localized "I". Self-talk supports the continuous stream of thoughts and ideas that flow through our minds and constantly refer back to an "I". Almost always critical in Westerners, the stream of self-reference leaps out of its accustomed channels when people recognize larger patterns. They begin to see themselves as part of something much larger than themselves.

Many mystics have been able to stabilize their pattern recognition capacity in such a way as to be able to see the underlying structure of the universe. Their recognition of the meta-pattern is rewarded by that flow of grace and energy described in mystical literature as rapture. When we shift to this mode, euphoria flows through the body in waves and subtle currents. (If you have ever had a sudden insight into the pattern of one of your problems, you have probably experienced a taste of this process.)

As we consider weather change, financial markets, technologies, and other interconnected structures and conditions, we are being pushed to consider global patterns and the effects they have on the lives of all living things and on the life and health of the planet itself. In effect we are being pushed to access our frontal lobe capacity — an adaptive and evolutionary challenge that requires us to literally retrain how we think and perceive. If we understand that we are being pushed to realize potentials already deep within our bodies and minds, then we will understand that our task is a spiritual practice as well as a response to external challenges. A prayer ascribed to St. Francis speaks to the transformation:

> Lord, make me an instrument of thy peace.
> Where there is hatred, let me sow love;
> Where there is injury, pardon;
> Where there is doubt, faith;

> Where there is despair, hope;
> Where there is darkness, light;
> Where there is sadness, joy.

From the perspective of brain function, St. Francis's prayer expresses an awakening of the higher faculties of the frontal lobes, and we need not ascribe to his version of faith to appreciate it. His prayer is not metaphoric nor a quaint appeal to a distant medieval God but an unlocking of the evolutionary potential that is the birthright of every human being. A sense of peace and joy, a profound capacity to forgive, concern for others, recognition of the patterns of global phenomena, and selfless action are the gifts of that unlocking.

Global change is midwifing a new way of seeing that recognizes the deepest currents of human experience and the stars of invariant truths burning in the fabric of our lives; it is birthing a way of seeing that intuitively informs us of right response. It is not easy to bring into the world a new way of seeing, of acting, and of living. An internal struggle takes place every day between old patterns of response and new patterns of soulful living.

We each risk rejection as we begin to respond to the dictates of our deeper selves. Most of us have learned to shield our light to make our way in the world: taunts from peers, put-downs from teachers or other adults, and control battles with parents often begin to intensify just as flashes of our depth and uniqueness emerge. However, I believe we are called upon as never before to unlock our evolutionary potential and reveal the light that lives within each of us.

To dance in the present we need to stay awake and to continually expand our own ability to recognize the large-scale patterns at work around us. The level of our response can transform fear into insight, depression into action, and doubt into faith. If we are willing to open our eyes, we will be given the grace to change our ways of comprehending the world. The challenge is before us. The response is ours to make.

Notes

1. Sound is synthesized by an interactive relationship between the environment, the ear, and the brain. More nerve endings originate in the brain and lead to the ear than originate in the ear and lead to the brain. Children who are musicians have a significantly more developed corpus collosum than do non-musicians. (The corpus collosum is the bundle of nerves that connects the two hemispheres of the brain.) A brain that easily communicates across the boundaries of the hemispheres is more likely to see the world in an integrated way.

At one level sound organizes matter — just think of how sound can draw large groups of people together. At another level sound is matter — everything vibrates at differing rates, making different sounds. When harmonious sound is made by our own voices or by sources around us, the effect on the physical structure of our bodies is immediate and palpable.

Additional Resources

INTERNET LINKS

http://media2.cs.berkeley.edu/webvideo/people/sandy/lobby.html
A remarkable visualization movie on the interaction of sound and matter (cynmatics) by Sandy Cohen.

http://www2.kpbsd.k12.ak.us/schools/northstar/NS.STAFF/GG/soumat.urls.html
A tutorial on sound and matter.

http://www.anthropressorg/press/shop/books/1582html
Ordering information for *Bringing Matter to Life with Sound*, a film by Dr. Hans Jenny and introduced by Dr. P. G. Ma. This film includes highlights of Dr. Jenny's pioneering experiments using audible sound to excite inert matter into lifelike, flowing forms. These delicate and intricate patterns demonstrate the responsiveness of all matter to its underlying vibrational tone. 30 min.,VHS Video.

http://www.tama-do.com/cells.html
A fascinating study of the effect of sound on cells; with pictures by Tama-do, Academy of Sound, Color, and Movement.

http://www.healing.about.com/health/healing/msubbodywork.htm
About.com site exploring various bodywork systems.

http://www.holisticmed.com/
Resources on holistic healing.

http://www.mareshbrainworks.com/B2B/SB12a.html
A simple and easy-to-access description of triune brain theory; with diagrams.

http://wwwkheper.auz.com/gaia/intelligence/MacLean.htm
A technical discussion of triune brain theory.

BOOKS

Bownds, M. Deric. *The Biology of Mind: Origins and Structures of Mind, Brain, and Consciousness.* Fitzgerald Science Press, 1999. ISBN 1891786075

Burger, Bruce. *Esoteric Anatomy: The Body As Consciousness.* North Atlantic Books, 1998. ISBN 1556432240

Castro, Miranda. *The Complete Homeopathy Handbook: A Guide to Everyday Health Care.* St. Martin's Press, 1991. ISBN 0312063202

Edwards, Betty. *The New Drawing on the Right Side of the Brain.* J P Tarcher, 1999. ISBN 0874774241

Frawley, David. *Ayurveda and the Mind: The Healing of Consciousness.* Lotus Light, 1997. ISBN 0914955365

Fugh-Berman M.D., Adriane. *Alternative Medicine: What Works — A Comprehensive, Easy-To-Read Review of the Scientific Evidence, Pro and Con.* Lippincott, Williams & Wilkins, 1997. ISBN 0683304070

Gardner, Howard E. *Art, Mind, and Brain: A Cognitive Approach to Creativity.* Basic Books, 1984. ISBN 0465004458

—————. *Creating Minds: An Anatomy of Creativity Seen Through the Lives of Freud, Einstein, Picasso, Stravinsky, Eliot, Graham, and Gandhi.* Basic Books, 1994. ISBN 0465014542

Gould, Stephen Jay. *Ontogeny and Phylogeny.* Belknap Press, 1985. ISBN 0674639413

Kloss, Jethro and Promise K. Moffet. *Back to Eden: A Human Interest Story of Health and Restoration to Be Found in Herb, Root, and Bark.* Lotus Press, 1988. Jethro Kloss Family Authorized Edition. ISBN 0940985098

Moss, Ralph W. *Alternative Medicine Online: A Guide to Natural Remedies on the Internet.* Equinox Press, 1997. ISBN 1881025101

Milne, Hugh. *Heart of Listening: A Visionary Approach to Craniosacral Work: Anatomy, Technique, Transcendence.* North Atlantic Books, 1998. ISBN 155643280

Pelletier, Kenneth R. *The Best Alternative Medicine: What Works? What Does Not?* Simon & Schuster, 2000. ISBN 0684842076

Whitmont, Edward C. *The Alchemy of Healing: Psyche and Soma.* North Atlantic Books, 1993. ISBN 1556431465

THE ROSE

Attar was a thirteenth-century healer from Persia,
who used the aromas of nature to help cure the body.
He was also a Sufi poet and mystic.
His most famous book, The Conference of Birds,
an allegorical tale describing the soul's journey,
is still read today. Attar reminds us
that the healing of the body is no different
than the healing of the soul.

The early memories come wrapped in heat. The beauty of something unseen fills my body and makes me glad to be alive. So it was that my first rose came to me by scent, in the beginning of the hot time when the rosebushes burst into bloom. I did not see its form, not then. And it is little matter that I was to discover the earthly source for its aroma, for something else had been awakened — a longing that would fill my heart.

Do you know that the essences of plants are like the gentle touches of an angel's wing? It is up to you whether or not you turn to see their beauty. I linger with many fragrances — with clove, myrrh, frankincense, orange flower, rose, and so many others. These are my friends, and they will help you, as well, if you open your heart to them. Sometimes as I pass my hands over the many perfumes that now dwell near me, I feel the rose blooming again in the chamber of my memory. I pray that I may never forget until the longing in my heart has finally brought me face-to-face with the Highest.

I know there are some who look down upon my profession as mere vanity. But if those skeptics could see the path of fragrance as I do, they would not deride me so. The unseen world touches this one in the center of the greatest beauties. Have you not watched the sunsets on the deserts as they meet the sea and felt the hand of Allah upon your shoulder? If you have not, then I fear that this world is a burden for you and not a pathway home.

The mystery of the rose set me upon my wanderings. I have been to Egypt, Damascus, Mecca, Turkestan, and India. The aroma of the unseen world has led me across many deserts and through the marketplaces of many cities. The knowledge I sought I could not find there, but much I learned I have gathered now about me.

Ah, the aromas I brought back! They are the guests who linger with me and remind me of the far-off places that I tested my soul to discover. For you see, the hidden hand of healing that brings relief from the pains of this world comes from a world beyond. It comes as an aroma on the winds of the soul.

You say I am healer? I say I am only answering the call of the unseen rose. A dream is like a scent in the night, is it not? And the lives of those who have gone before us, do they not leave an odor in the air? The saints, they leave the sweet fragrance of life burnt through to the pure clean lines of a rose. This I know because I have met them in my dreams. Al-Hallaj came to me one night and whispered with a roar into my ears, "I am the truth." It was the very saying for which he was killed.

Many need truth kept far from them so that they might not have to burn with its fire. It scares them when it comes near. And when the breath of a saint is felt, though the scent be sweet, the fire burns hot. That is why, I am sure, they killed my gentle friend of the night — Al-Hallaj. He had burnt himself through until he was the truth. It may sound like blasphemy to those who want their God comfortably distant, but those who long for truth itself will, in the end, become that which they seek.

I have risked much to speak of the worlds beyond the edge of this one. Sometimes I think that this fever which

consumes me and makes me write is coming from an unfriend-
ly flower, so much trouble has it brought. I have tried to close
the door and hold back the words. But that is not possible. I
was born to follow the scent of a flower I cannot see.

I wonder why it is, sometimes, that people long to be free
of their pain yet fear the very means to gain their freedom.
Their fear has killed other lovers of the unseen world, and it
has stolen my worldly goods from me and sent me into exile.
Their fear has tried to silence my writings. But it will not work.

Have you ever tried to wipe away an odor of garlic?
Or banish onions from your body? Can you keep the fields of
poppies from lulling you to sleep when they are in bloom?
Can you make a rose stop spreading its beauty in the wind?

Chapter Twelve

12

INDESTRUCTIBLE BODIES AND
AGENTS OF CHANGE

Assisi in the thirteenth century was a small, walled city perched on the edge of Mount Subasio. Within the safety of its walls the citizens of Assisi worked, played, prayed, and argued much as anyone in any community anywhere at just about any time. People worried about keeping warm through the winters and they argued over bad debts. They grumbled about the garrison of German soldiers who lived in the castle above town and the petty dictators who seemed to rotate in and out of service there. They welcomed the emissaries of the Pope, who arrived with a flurry of colorful vestments and incense. The parade of color amidst the stone walls and streets of Assisi was a welcome respite from the drudgery of everyday tasks.

One day a curious crowd gathered in one of the town plazas to watch a bellicose father and his thin, short son arguing before the bishop of Assisi. The son was determined to give away all of his parent's wealth to the poor. The father thought his son was ungrateful and that he had lost his reason. In a symbolic gesture of disdain the son stripped the clothes from his back, announcing that he was now in God's hands. The bishop of Assisi is said to have used his own robes to cover Francesco's nakedness. But there was nothing the bishop could do to hide the radical faith that had suddenly begun to burn in the young man's heart.

Francesco left his old life behind and wandered the hillsides, living in the forests around Assisi. He had a deep appreciation for hard work, loved to sing, and was very suspicious of book learning. Above all he had an irrepressible faith in a world not easily seen. In an era that was rife with conflict and change, Francesco — better known as St. Francis of Assisi — lived life according to the dictates of his faith. His life inspired then and continues to inspire now.

Voices in every age have risen above the wars, politics, struggles, and trials of life to sound a call. These voices challenge us to examine the limits we impose upon ourselves; they urge us to join in the fire of transcendence; and they ask us to put aside our cynical judgments and to trust in love. Whose are these voices? They are the voices of mystics, those beings whose lives give visible expression to the realm of the spirit.

Mystics have been men and women, rich and poor, young and old. They have appeared on every continent during every age. Many lived obscure lives, unnoticed by the stream of history; others were propelled to the forefront of their cultures.

Mystics and their seemingly miraculous manifestations consistently overturn our expectations and understanding of the world. Matter, energy, time, space, and causation all undergo radical shifts in the presence of these beings. Our material world is literally transformed. These beings tend to rearrange the age they live in, the people whose lives they touch, and even the substance of their own bodies.

Consider this story from India (which is considered there to be a factual account). A yogi was meditating at the tomb of a revered saint who had died many hundreds of years ago. In the course of the meditation the saint appeared to the yogi and said, "I am strangling. You must help me."

In his inner vision the yogi saw an image of the saint with a vine growing around his neck, so he went to the guardians of the tomb and reported what he had heard and seen. The guardians, knowing how worlds interpenetrate, carefully removed the stone lid to the tomb and found the body of Janeshwar, still fully intact, sitting in the meditation pose in which he had been buried. Curled around his neck was a vine that had grown up from the earth beneath the tomb. The guardians cleared away the vine and resealed the tomb.

We could dismiss this story as legend if it were not for a story from modern times that has been fully verified as true. In 1952 the body of Swami Yogananda — mystic and yogi — was brought to Forest Lawn (a cemetery east of Los Angeles) and was laid to rest with reverence, perhaps even with a quality of devotion. A month later the director of Forest Lawn issued a notarized letter, in which he testified that after 20 days the body showed no visible signs of decay — in his experience, a unique circumstance.[1]

Numerous claims can be made about interior experiences that may or may not be true, but bodies do not lie. Indestructible bodies present a difficult conundrum for those who would deny that shifts in consciousness can directly affect matter. How, for instance, does one account for the lack of cellular degeneration — something that seemingly violates all known biological processes? Mystics such as Yogananda have burned through the fabric of this world with their intensity, will, and unbounded energy. They live in the radiance of what is possible and often manifest effects far beyond our everyday understanding. These are not tame lives.

Yogananda was saved from two cases of deadly Asiatic cholera through the intervention of grace. He had excruciating headaches for many years and chronic digestive disorders throughout his adolescence, both of which he overcame as a result of miraculous healing. He went on to become a tireless traveler, crisscrossing the United States in the 1920s and 1930s, speaking to tens of thousands of people and creating one of the first bridges between Indian mystical tradition and the West.

St. Francis completed at least six forty-day fasts in the wilderness. Ramakrishna, an Indian saint, spent weeks at a time without sleep as the fire of spiritual processes coursed through his body.

St. Teresa of Avila suffered from a lifetime of physical maladies, including one episode when for four days she was thought to be dead. She awoke to find her eyelids waxed together in preparation for burial. After regaining consciousness, she remained paralyzed for three years, yet she went on to become a tireless administrator of her new order, traveling continuously and experiencing raptures and spiritual ecstasies.

St. Catherine of Sienna lived the last years of her life eating only an occasional communion wafer and barely sleeping. All the while she was healing plague victims and working actively to return the Pope from Avignon to Rome.

And Rumi, the Persian mystic, was forced to flee his childhood home and had to suffer the death of his beloved teacher Shams at the hands of his followers. Yet he went on to guide his community with courage, compassion, and grace during the difficult years of the Mongol invasions.

The personalities of these mystics are not tame either. St. Francis forbade his brothers to store up even a day's supply of grain because it showed a lack of faith in providence. Ramakrishna slapped his benefactor for worrying about a lawsuit while the man stood in front of an altar. St. Catherine of Sienna chided popes and emperors, had little patience with bureaucrats, and cowed most of the men who met her by the force of her will. And Yogananda had a fierce temper, as those close to him sometimes discovered.

The stories of the mystics are shells we pick up along the shore of the spiritual ocean; hold them to our ears and we will hear the roar of the sea. I must warn you that contemplating the lives of these beings is fundamentally dangerous. Their stories will uproot your complacency and challenge your assumptions of what is possible. They might even inspire you to wake in the early morning hours and dance under the morning star. In the end you will go beyond all stories, all reports.

It is not easy for us to hear about mystics, for in contemplating their paths we must inevitably confront the question "Why not us?" St. Francis encountered Christ during a mountain fast and St. Teresa of Avila experienced raptures so blissful that she would rise physically from the earth. Ramakrishna could remain in a superconscious state for days at a time and Yogananda could still his bodily functions and merge into bliss at will.

If we take the path of cowardice we will reduce the testimony of these saints and mystics to mere superstition and derangement. If we take the path of weakness we will make them gods and goddesses by assuming that we can never approach their experiences. If we take the path of courage we will ask, "How might we become what we have heard?"

I consider the mystics of the world our premier agents of change. Though inventors, scientists, artists, merchants, warriors, and healers have effected and continue to effect great planetary change, it is the mystics who change the structure of matter itself. If we are truly to understand change we would do well to consider their lives and teachings.

Mystics act as guides. Most of us feel a restlessness, a spirit of adventure that pushes us toward new horizons, toward Goethe's "new fields of life exploring." If we understand this fundamental urge as one that can guide us through trials, changes, and disruptions and toward the realization of our full potential, then we will have a much different response to dislocations than will people who do not have that understanding.

Whenever cynicism threatens to overwhelm our hearts, or when our imaginations feel insipid and dry, we can keep company with the most inspired of friends. Gandhi had the poems of Mirabai (a favorite saint) read often in his ashrams. He drew great sustenance from both the reality of her life and the mythic power of her story. Our minds become that which they dwell upon. By uplifting our minds with inspiring stories, we can cultivate an open door to the fundamentals of life.

As we listen with "the ears of our hearts" we can actually change our consciousness. Because language is so fundamental to thought and thought is so crucial to the unfolding of consciousness, it makes intuitive sense that language ought to be able to accelerate our transformation. There are whole sciences dedicated to the transformation of awareness through the specific sounds and functions of language. Sanskrit and Hebrew, for example, have both been used with great precision for this purpose. Mystics also give us a sense of the humanly possible. When the outer world manifests discontinuity and change, the field of experience opens to core levels of reality. If we condition ourselves to the interior world, we will be better prepared to encounter that world as it breaks through in the abrupt shifts of outer events. As the phenomena of indestructible bodies attest, mystics are able to transcend the limits of physicality as a result of the depth of their penetration into the unseen world of the spirit.

Indestructible bodies are not the only effects mystics are able to manifest. Padre Pio, a modern-day mystic, manifested a phenomenon known as bilocation on numerous occasions.[2] He was seen to appear at the bedsides of terminally ill patients (who then were mysteriously healed) while never having left his monastery in southern Italy. (Documentation of these events is extensive.) In Eastern traditions bilocation is considered one of several siddhis (powers) that advanced yogis can manifest.

When the Karmappa, one of the principal Buddhist teachers of our times, was dying in a Chicago Hospital, he manifested a series of cancers one after another with a rapidity that defied medical understanding. His intent was to aid the alleviation of suffering that cancer has brought to the world. Some witnesses claimed that he manifested all known cancers in the course of his dying (though this particular claim was unverified).

Finally, mystics demonstrate a coherence that helps re-order the world. When important work is set in motion, two contradictory forces are activated: resistance to the change and support from unseen realms. Focused attention that serves a greater good creates a coherence that organizes the world into an active body of help. I use the term "body of help" very deliberately here. In mystics such as Padre Pio the body of help literally materialized in a physical form; in other situations and instances it will appear as a subtle intervention of support.

I am going to suggest that when we bring together our focused intent with emotional passion and energy we, too, invoke that body of help. Ernest Shackleton, whom we met earlier in this book, spoke candidly of receiving ongoing guidance from another realm as he shepherded his men through the grueling trial of the loss of the Endurance. In a more recent and very down-to-earth example, some Russian émigrés decided to open a bakery in the heart of Seattle's Pike Street Market. They had next to no money, but they did have a clear intention, expertise, and a sincere love of baking. A space came open at the market, and as they were agonizing over how to achieve their goal, a local restaurateur delivered a large check to their door, simply because he believed in them and their dream — a most immediate and tangible expression of a body of help.

In the end the stories of the mystics circle around one center, and their challenge is a simple yet profound one: we are asked to trust in love. Our willingness to bring forth the subtle fields of our deepest hopes and inspirations links our lives to those of the mystics of all ages who have chosen the same course. And our belief in the power of imagination and in the daring of the human heart can and does literally rearrange the physical world, making everyday life a mystical process.

Notes

1. See Paramahansa Yogananda, *Autobiography of a Yogi* (Self-Realization Fellowship, 1981).

2. See Bernard C. Ruffin, *Padre Pio: The True Story* (Our Sunday Visitor, 1991).

Additional Resources

INTERNET LINKS

http://www.yogananda-srf.org/
The home page of the Self-Realization Fellowship (the center founded by Swami Yogananda).

http://www.ananada.org/
Ananda's homepage, founded by J. Donald Walters, a disciple of Swami Yogananda; includes an on-line version of Yogananda's famous *Autobiography of a Yogi*.

http://c-level.com/milarepa/
A delightful version of Milarepa's life in pictures by Eva van Dam.

http://www.cosmicharmony.com/Av/Milarepa/Milarepa.htm
An excellent account of Milarepa's life with some illustrations.

http://timesofchange.org/st.htm.
The author's version of St. Teresa of Avila.

http://tidesofchange.org/mirabai.htm
The author's page on Mirabai.

http://www.catholic-forum.com/churches/296stteresa/history.htm
A short history of St. Teresa of Avila.

http://www.padrepio.com/
A source for material on Padre Pio.

http://www.ramakrishna.org/
A source for material on Ramakrishna.

http://www.ramakrishnamath-mlore.org/index.html
Further source material on Ramakrishna.

http://www.gobindsadan.org/healing/glimpses/index.shtml
Access to information about a variety of mystics and prophets.

http://www.newadvent.org/cathen/03447a.htm
Biography of St. Catherine of Sienna in the *Catholic Encyclopedia*.

BOOKS

Alston, A.J. *Devotional Poems of Mirabai*. South Asia Books, 1980. ISBN 8120804414 Out of print.

Andrae, Tor. *Mohammed the Man and His Faith*. Ayer, 1971. ISBN 0836958217

Armstrong, Karen. *Muhammad: Biography of the Prophet*. Harper San Francisco, 1993. ISBN 0062508865

Barks, Coleman and John Moyne, Trans. *The Essential Rumi*. Harper San Francisco, 1997 ISBN 0062509594

Cohen, J.M., Trans. *The Life of Saint Teresa of Avila by Herself*. Penguin USA, 1988. ISBN 0140440739

Harlan, Lindsey. *Religion and Rajput Women: The Ethic of Protection in Contemporary Narratives*. University of California Press, 1992. ISBN 0520073398

——————— , author; and Paul B. Courtright, editor. *From the Margins of Hindu Marriage*. Oxford University Press, 1995. ISBN 0195081188 [Note: See chapter "Abandoning Shame: Mira on the Margins of Marriage," which works well with John Hawley's Chapter 5 on Mirabai in *Songs of the Saints of India*.]

Hawley, John Stratton and Mark Juergensmeyer. *Songs of the Saints of India*. Oxford University Press, 1988. ISBN 0195052218

Hixon, Lex. *Great Swan: Meetings with Ramakrishna*. Larson Publications, 1997. ISBN 0943914809

Isherwood, Christopher. *Ramakrishna and His Disciples*. Vedanta Press, 1980. ISBN 087481037X

Mi-La-Ras-Pa, author; and Garma C. C. Chang, translator. *The Hundred Thousand Songs Of Milarepa: The Life-Story and Teaching of the Greatest Poet-Saint Ever to Appear in the History of Buddhism*. Shambhala, 1999. ISBN 1570624763

——————— , Lama Kunga Rinpoche, author; and Brian Cutillo, translator. *Drinking the Mountain Stream: Songs of Tibet's Beloved Saint, Milarepa: Eighteen Selections from the Rare Collection: Stories and Songs*. Wisdom Publications, 1995. ISBN 0861710630

Ramakrishna, author; and Swami Nikhilananda, translator. *The Gospel of Sri Ramakrishna*. Ramakrishna Vivekanada Center, 1985. ISBN 0911206019

Ruffin, Bernard C. *Padre Pio: The True Story*. Our Sunday Visitor, 1991. ISBN 0879736739

Rumi, Jalal Al-Din, author; and Coleman Barks, translator. *The Glance: Songs of Soul-Meeting*. Viking Press, 1999. ISBN 0670887552

——————— , author; and Nader E. Khalili, translator. Rumi, *Fountain of Fire*. Cal-Earth Press, 1996. ISBN 1889625035

Schimmel, Annemarie. *I Am Wind You Are Fire: The Life and Work of Rumi*. Shambhala, 1992. ISBN 1570626456

St. Teresa of Avila, author; and E. Allison Peers, translator. *Interior Castle*. Image Books, 1972. ISBN 0385036434

Yogananda, Paramahansa and W. Y. Evans-Wentz (Preface). *Autobiography of a Yogi*. Self-Realization Fellowship, 1979. ISBN 0876120796

THE HAILSTORM

The life of Milarepa, one of Tibet's most beloved mystics,
is a classic redemption story. As a young man he learned
black magic and supposedly caused many deaths in the service
of his mother's vengeance. Repenting of his crimes, he sought
out the wisdom of a teacher who had brought the teachings
of the Buddha to Tibet, and he spent many years meditating
in caves, subsisting on almost nothing. Milarepa followed
the difficult path of inner work and achieved an exalted state.
Though his path is not for everyone, his capacity to
transform himself is an inspiration to all.

The hailstorm had come and gone. I was pleased to see the blue sky once again. Hailstorms had a way of making me nervous. Too often they reminded me of the black magic I had used to invoke them and of the deaths I had caused with them. Today I greeted the storm without any hardening of my heart. For what had been revealed to me in the depths of my nightly meditation still lingered with the coming of the morning.

The sun began to reflect from off the many moistened stones that fell away from the cave opening. I closed my eyes, tipped my head back, and let the sun fill my face. In the reverie of warmth, with fresh hail still melting, I recalled my teacher Marpa and what he had shared. He told me that the seeds of conscious experiences live embedded in the central column of light within my body. The past vexes us all, and none more than myself. He said that the seeds of the past are passed down through the generations and the lifetimes of our experience. And he spoke of the delicate task of burning through these seeds without opening them.

"Mila, my fine magician," he said to me one day, "the art of a meditator is to find a way to offer up our bodies and minds without opening the seeds of our past. For every seed that opens must be lived out in our lives through our karma. It is one of the most delicate of balances that we are asked to undertake in recovering our Buddha nature, this burning of seeds without bursting them."

For some reason as he spoke, an image appeared within my mind of the barley my mother had burnt so long ago. It was the very day she had sent me in search of magic to fulfill her vengeance. She heard me singing as I came back from a wedding and was so angry at hearing my happy voice raised in song that she fainted dead away. I carried her into the house, and as I put her down on some cushions I noticed the burnt barley.

Burning one's barley is a serious matter to us Tibetans. We do not have the kind of surplus most of you lowland dwellers are used to. To burn even the smallest portion of our beloved grain is a sign of ill will to come. And my mother had burnt many a barley seed that day. The charred remains of their husks still smelled of scorched wrath.

I could not get the image of those blackened husks out of my mind. For many long weeks and even years as I came near to grasping the full meaning of Marpa's words, the blackened hulls of my mother's barley would appear and block me on my journey. I despaired of ever moving past those husks. Until last night.

In the quiet hours of darkness during my midnight meditation when only the stars were awake, I slipped past the blackened hulls and found the seeds of my memories. A current of light moved through my body and began to boil the seeds away, diminishing each one until it became a small light, a small star in the blackness of the cave. So it was that today I greeted the hailstorm without any hardening of my heart. My meditation had shown me the balance Marpa had spoken about.

You ask how I would know that a storm was coming? I tell you, ever since I learned to summon storms and use them against people I have had an uncommon communion with the weather, and I know when hail is on its way. I am grateful that I remain in close contact with the weather and take it as a sign that the elements have forgiven me for my past abuses. The steam rising from the landscape before me is like a prayer rising back to the heavens.

Only Tibet can be so clean after a storm. Sunlight stretches before me all the way to the distant peaks. The Buddha realms themselves seem visible in the charged purity of the air. I often fancy that the changing of the sky and the retiring of the clouds are the gestures of the Buddha's blessing. And I understand why it is said that on the second watch of the Buddha's enlightenment he witnessed many hundreds of thousands of his former lives — he had been burning the seeds of his past to clear the space of his present.

Chapter Thirteen

13

TRUSTING BEYOND THE OBVIOUS AND LAYING STONES FOR THE FUTURE

I know, Your Honor, that every atom of life in all this universe is

bound up together. I know that a pebble cannot be thrown into the ocean

without disturbing every drop of water in the sea. I know that every life

is inextricably mixed and woven with every other life. I know that every

influence, conscious and unconscious, acts and reacts on every living

organism, and that no one can fix the blame.

— Clarence Darrow

CLARENCE DARROW made this eloquent statement during a sensational murder trial in the late 1920s. As a child Darrow had watched the burial of a Union soldier and had experienced an overwhelming terror of death on that occasion. His experience may help explain why he became an ardent opponent of capital punishment and why he said that he would die himself if any of his clients were to receive the death penalty. (None of them ever did.) He reached national fame defending a teacher in Tennessee for teaching evolution in the schools. Though he was a confirmed agnostic,

Darrow's awareness of the greater web of being underlay and informed his actions. He was a man of sharp and decisive ability who used his power to declare and uphold the connectivity of the individual to the collective. And he trusted in the existence of a power much greater than his own.

The web of being is not just an intuition of spiritual reality but, as we have seen, has scientific support and is found in the practical world of human events as well. The intelligence that knits together this universe is just that — intelligent. And if that is so, what action is required of us?

Consider the Lord's Prayer. The third line of this well-known prayer reads, "Thy kingdom come." In the original Aramaic (the language Christ spoke), malkutakh means both 'fruitful arm' and 'kingdom' — a dual meaning that conveys both the creative potential inherent in the Earth itself as well as that waiting to be unfolded by human action. Malkatuh (from the same root) shares connotations with the word for "Great Mother" — the concept name given by many preliterate cultures to refer to their experience and understanding of the world as interconnected body. The kingdom of which Christ spoke, therefore, is tied to the realization (the making real) of the inherent consciousness of the universe. And its coming has to do with a human awakening to the very reality experienced by mystics and described by scientists.

Most spiritual traditions speak of the need to surrender to the will of a greater aspect of creation. Unfortunately, because of the horrendous abuses made in the name of religion, the true meaning of surrender has been lost or obscured, and so when we discuss or contemplate our spiritual surrender we need to use our powers of discernment. To surrender does not mean that we give over the integrity of our beings to another person or organization. (The imperative to surrender is sometimes appropriated by various power structures and made into laws that are then violently enforced. The Inquisitors who tried Galileo as a heretic were early enforcers for the power structure of the Catholic Church. In a more recent example women in Afghanistan are currently being tortured or stoned to death by order of male religious authorities for offenses as trivial as exposing their arms.) To surrender means to release the identification we have with self-protection and our own personal dramas and to find a greater identity in the whole of creation.

Trust is fundamental to the process of surrender. Without trust we will be unable to give ourselves up to the infinite subtleties of the whole, since our habitual strategies of protection will constantly override any messages we receive. That being said, we all have the capacity to hear and respond to the voice of the whole.

Most indigenous people will tell you that every location, every part of the Earth, has a spirit and is sacred. They would also say that this sacredness can be intuited and can directly influence our choices. We can all learn from this wisdom.

A few years ago I led a retreat for some Native Aleut men. We camped at the head of the bay away from the distractions and habits of village life. As we gathered in a circle the morning following our first night out, one of the men who held a position of importance in the village seemed agitated and out of sorts. I asked him what was wrong. He said he hadn't slept well, that the Earth had been angry with him all night, filling his sleep with bad dreams. The anger, he explained, was because of a decision he had helped make to cut trees for profit around the village.

When the Aleut man said that the Earth was angry with him he wasn't just talking metaphorically. The distress in his eyes told me he was, indeed, experiencing the anguish of his decision as an emanation of the ground on which he had slept. In his sleep he had listened to the wisdom of the whole that was asking him to change his behavior, to surrender personal desire for a larger good. The web of creation had spoken to the man directly.

If we look back in the history of Christianity, St. Francis provides us with a clear example of someone who trusted implicitly in the underlying supportive fabric of creation. A few short years after Francis began speaking of his inner experience, five thousand

Brothers were arriving from all over Italy to the woods that Francis and his small band called home. The magnetism of Francis's conviction had reached into the impoverished lives of Italy's residents and called them to a new level of response.

St. Dominic, a fastidious, disciplined man with a highly developed attention to detail was one of the men who gathered in the woods. (The positive attributes of discipline, order, and asceticism that became the hallmark of the Dominican order would later mutate into the ruthlessness associated with the Inquisition, with which the Dominicans were intimately involved.) When St. Dominic saw the hordes of men arriving by the hour he turned to St. Francis and chided him, saying, "Have you not prepared to house and feed all these men? It is irresponsible not to tend to their needs."

Francis replied that he trusted that the Lord would take care of the situation. When pushed, Francis would only say, "Wait and see."

Shortly afterward, wagons full of food and bedding began to appear. From communities all along the Spoleto Valley came an outpouring of spontaneous generosity that would take care of the five thousand Brothers.

St. Dominic was apologetic. "I have not had enough faith. I am sorry. You have shown the way, Brother Francis."

I like this story because it shows providence at work, but it also shows that results come from the seeds of action that we sow. St. Francis gave of himself selflessly, preaching in small town squares throughout the area. He tended the lepers and was notorious for giving away his father's wealth to worthy causes. His generosity seeded the garden of response in the hearts of his countrymen.

If the web of connection supporting our world is to leap up into recognizable shape, we need to take selfless action. The many problems facing our modern world will not be solved by the intervention of fate but by effort and grace. By serving the good of the whole, we are served ourselves — a simple but profoundly important principle. Many times our acts will bring about unexpected consequences. Consider the following story.

A farmer in Scotland was out working his fields when he heard a cry from the bogs. He raced toward the sounds of distress and found a boy, mired in the mud and sinking fast. He pulled him to safety and, after comforting him, sent him on his way.

The next day, a coach pulled up at the farmer's home and a nobleman, the father of the boy the farmer had saved, stepped down to greet him. The nobleman offered him a reward, but the farmer would have none of it. The nobleman insisted. The two haggled back and forth until they struck a deal: the nobleman would pay for the education of the farmer's son.

The farmer's son, Alexander Fleming, went to medical school and, after graduating, became the man who discovered penicillin. Fleming's discovery was to save the life of the nobleman's son one more time. When Winston Churchill — for he was the nobleman's son — contracted pneumonia, penicillin saved his life.

Life is a symbol. If we move deeply into its heart with courage and integrity, then we begin to see the world as sacred, as a co-evolving and intelligent field of being out of which events arise, giving structure and guidance to our lives. To trust is to experience the world as sacred. We will not discover this sacredness unless we risk relationship. And in order to risk relationship, we must trust.

We have all had the experience of trusting in someone or something that let us down, disappointed, or perhaps even betrayed us. Sometimes we may unconsciously project our need out into the world, hoping other people will magically transform our inner experience. When we find ourselves feeling let down our tendency may be to withdraw from engaging fully in life again.

Betrayals do not mean that life is not sacred; they only mean that we are putting our trust in unreliable sources. As many of life's most painful lessons teach, whenever we expect someone or something else to do our work for us, we will be disappointed and even embittered. When we assume responsibility for our own journey, the hand of guidance that steers us will be felt as both our own and not our own — its movement in our lives a mysterious marriage of the personal and the impersonal.

Too many of our habitual practices are based on the arrogant assumption that there is no problem that we cannot rationally solve. But real solutions to our problems depend on a broader definition of problem-solving that includes a subtle understanding of the connection we each have to the web of life. We must at least be willing to listen to the voice of conscience, as the Aleut man did — even if that conscience seems to speak from the Earth itself. Our willingness to follow the thread of guidance as it appears in subtle form in our lives will help bring about the full realization of both outer and inner worlds.

Consider the story of the lovely retreat site — dedicated to all religions — which is located near the end of Sunset Boulevard in Los Angeles. Paramahansa Yogananda, the well-known yogi from India, had been wanting to find some land on which to build a retreat center away from the bustle of downtown Los Angeles. One day he received a letter from a stranger who offered to give him a parcel of land with a small lake near the ocean.

The man shared that, while he had been staying with his wife near the lake, he had been awakened three times in one night by the same incredibly vivid dream, in which he was shown that the piece of land he owned was to be made into a church for all religions. The next day the man looked in the phone book, searching for such a church. The Self Realization Fellowship, which spoke of the universality of all religions, was the entry that came closest to what he had been shown. He was so moved by his dreams that he decided to donate the land to the church, and he mailed a letter off with his offer. His wife thought him crazy, but the Lake Shrine stands today as a symbol of what can happen when the inner world, on the wings of inspiration and dreams, takes form in the outer world.

Let me tell you a story about a revolution. This revolution was not planned, and no violence was used. It began, in fact, with the simplest of acts. One day Brother Francis passed a run-down church on the plains below Assisi.

Francis felt called to enter the church and pray. Prayer, for Francis, was not the pious execution of a few rote lines but an utter abandonment to the act of praying. It was his passion. So he went inside the church.

As he prayed he heard the crucifix say to him, "Brother Francis, as you see, my church is in disrepair. Please rebuild it."

Now if you or I were to hear a crucifix talking, we might well label ourselves delusional and seek a quick exit. But Francis was a different man and he lived in different times. He took the words as a command and began to rebuild the church of San Damiano stone by stone. As he labored he was joined by others who were attracted to his simple joy, love of song, and obvious spiritual intoxication. In a few short years their community had grown to include five thousand Brothers.

Francis's obedience to an inner prompting, no matter how ridiculous it may have seemed, launched a revolution. The revolution was not about putting stones upon stones, though the revolution could not have come about without those actions. The revolution was about the emergence of a spiritual renaissance that would blossom and grow until it reached full flower in the efflorescence of humanism that began in Florence, Italy, and spread throughout Europe during the fourteenth to sixteenth centuries. Francis changed religious practice to support the personal empowerment of the individual and gave new hope to an entire sector of society that previously had been disenfranchised. When Francis laid the first stone at the church of San Damiano he was laying stones for the future — a future that no one could have foreseen.

Some four centuries later, in India, a man picked up a simple object and began to spin the fabric of another revolution. Gandhi wanted to find a way to inspire self-respect in the common people of India. He was looking for a way to overturn India's reliance on British-made cloth and, by extension, to overturn British political and economic control. When Gandhi began to spin his own cloth he was exercising a spiritual muscle but in a very concrete way. Spinning became one of the enduring symbols of his revolution — a revolution that freed India and proved nonviolent action to be a viable tool for achieving transformation.

Deep in the southern United States in the 1800's, when slavery was still the law of the land, a man picked up a scrap of paper and began the difficult task of trying to make sense of the letters and words he saw. Frederick Douglass, through his own intense effort and against active persecution, taught himself how to read and write — skills that were winnowed out of the fields of his toil and imprisonment. He took his skill with language to the national stage, and the clear and precise prose of his courage helped to guide our nation through a Civil War. The act was simple, but the will behind the act helped transform a nation.

There have been many stone layers throughout history, but there was only one St. Francis. Cloth has been woven for centuries, but it took a Gandhi to spin a revolution. The written word has been handed down for generations, but it took a Frederick Douglass to express what a nation needed to hear in a time of pain and loss. In all three men the marriage of inner work with simple outer actions brought about enormous changes in the world. Like them, our own willingness to marry our inner voice of guidance to our skills will pave the way for a true revolution in our lives and in our world.

Each of us possesses skills. When we are called upon to change, we need not build cathedrals overnight. Individual actions, taken one at a time in the reverence of our attention, will help us lay stones for our future. As the props of our material world are undergoing waves of stress from many points of disturbance, we need to pick up the stones of a revolution and build a simpler, kinder way of living and live quieter, more meaningful lives.

We are called upon to give our world the tender healing of our undivided attention. Such focus is the essence of simplicity, for in the act of devoted attention we render the world sacred. The most powerful antidote to the discontinuities of change is our capacity to reach through the shifting flux of our lives and make holy each moment with simple, undivided attention. By joining with others in a simplicity of attention and action we look beyond the debris, fluctuations, and confusion of the exterior world and make visible the worlds that live as hopes within our deepest hearts. We can, in the waves of world forming, become agents of change ourselves, co-creators of a new world.

Additional Resources

INTERNET LINKS

http://www.law.umkc.edu/faculty/projects/FTRIALS/leoploeb/LEOPOLD.htm
  Information and quotes from the Leopold Loeb trial.

http://www.elohi.com/photo/assisi/
  A photo-essay on Assisi by Jay Pulli.

http://www.assisi.com/index.html
  A guide to the art, history, and environment of Assisi.

http://www.newadvent.org/cathen/06221a.htm
  A biography of St. Francis in the Catholic Encyclopedia.

BOOKS

Chesterton, G. K. *St. Francis of Assisi*. Image Books, 1987. ISBN 0385029004

Gandhi, Mahatma. *An Autobiography: The Story of My Experiments with Truth*. Translated by Mahadev Desai. Beacon Press, 1993. ISBN 0807059099

Green, Julien and Peter Heinegg. *God's Fool: The Life and Times of Francis of Assisi*. Harper San Francisco, 1987. ISBN 0060634642

Heywood, W., ed. *The Little Flowers of St. Francis of Assisi*. Vintage Books, 1998. Vintage Spiritual Classics. Preface by Madeleine L'Engle. ISBN 037570020X

McMichaels, Susan W. *Journey Out of the Garden: St. Francis of Assisi and the Process of Individuation*. Paulist Press, 1997. ISBN 0809137267

A DAMASCUS MORNING

*Ibn Arabi joins St. Francis, Rumi, and others as yet
another member of the companions of the thirteenth century who
manifested a remarkable spiritual renaissance in the midst of
tumultuous times. A controversial figure (rejected to this day
by the more conservative arms of Islam), Arabi was born in 1165
in Murcia, Spain. He underwent a spontaneous mystical opening
at the age fifteen that was to be tempered by contact with many
of the greatest teachers of his time — over ninety by Arabi's own
count. Credited with more than 850 books, the breadth, depth,
and fullness of Arabi's vision reformulated much of the
metaphysics of Sufism. The two deepest streams of his life appear
to be the ongoing mystical openings that evolved over his lifetime
and the remarkable acumen of his mind. He was, as were many
of the Sufis, a poet as well. Ibn Arabi died in Damascus in 1240.*

"The Prophet came to me last night," he announced as
we walked over the flagstones toward the arches of
his private chambers. Far off, across the hillsides, the call to
prayer floated out across the waiting world.

He had come at last to Damascus, his wandering over.
Each morning he rose and prayed. Before taking his morning

meal he would often reflect on the day's inspiration or speak, as he did today, of a dream that had come with the night.

"And . . .?" I asked.

"He held a book in His hands and asked me to listen as He read the title. *Fusus Al-Hikam, (The Gems of the Wisdom of the Prophets)* were the words He spoke. And in His quiet way, I knew He meant for me to write such a book for the benefit of my students."

"Another book?" I asked.

He knew from my tone that I did not approve. And he was right. I saw the toll each book took as he began to ride yet another wave of inspiration, though I marveled at the ocean that continuously revealed itself through his mind, heart, and pen.

"You worry, don't you?" he asked.

"I do, for the light of your books seems to be a torch to your body. Have you not just healed from your long disease?"

"Bismillah . . . It is in Allah's hands." And he raised his hands, palms up toward the sky, as he spoke.

"But, surely, you have some say, for it is your hands as well which do the writing."

"You would turn the Prophet from your dreams?"

He had me there. Of course I wouldn't.

"When I write," he continued in his beautifully modulated voice, " it is Allah, speaking through the Angel of Inspiration, who is doing the writing. I could no more turn aside such a visitation than I could stay the morning sun as it warms our lands."

"But, surely, you have some say in all of this? Where is the tenderness of your human self to find its placement?"

"I have been given a full life, and I have years yet to live. Do not worry yourself."

In this he was right, for indeed, he lived another ten years past our conversation that morning. But I know in my heart that he would have been with us many more years if the Angel of Inspiration had not visited him so many times. But then we cannot tell the ocean how to flow; the best we can do is bow in respect as the waters move according to a greater will.

That morning, as the sun began to warm the air, the birds tucked away their songs and the sounds of our awakening community filled the air. I found great comfort in that waking, for it gave my mind something other than the Angel's hand to think about for a moment.

He noticed my pause and read it, as he always did, exactly for what it was.

"The awakened heart is no longer the sovereign of its own domain. You must know this by now, my friend."

I did not really have words with which to respond.

"The Angel of Inspiration is a visitor who is more conscious than the host, for She knows and understands the light of Allah and how that light is to be shared. We can set the table and open the doors and lay out the meal, but once the guest has come, we cannot presume to tell Her how to live Her life. This would be most unkind and it would show a lack of faith."

"Must we just submit?"

"What is the meaning of Islam?" he countered.

And, again, he had me there. Of all the many men and women I had met in my long life, he lived a life of most exalted submission. I knew that his very act of submitting was the key to his remarkable productivity; and I also knew — because I had seen it in a vision — that what he brought forth was to water the future ages.

"You would like me to keep a small bit of myself safe, would you not?" he asked. "Perhaps find a harbor for me to rest in for a while. It is kind that you should want this for me. I know that it is an expression of your love, but I ask you to feel into the heart behind the heart."

As he spoke, a strange mood came over me. My heart felt as if were taken out of my body. It felt enormous, larger than the room in which we stood, larger than the sounds of the waking city, larger even than the light streaming from the warming sun. Instead of observing myself from the usual anchor point of my mind, I was aware of myself as a wave, as part of the vast ocean from which the Angel of Inspiration itself came.

I had the peculiar sensation that our conversation had already occurred, that my worry and concern for my friend was a wave from the same ocean as his ecstatic illumination. I saw, then, that the divine presence did not have the capacity to diminish itself. Wherever channels are open, rivers of light pour through, deepening always the groove of their passage into the relative world.

I felt simultaneously powerless and completely empowered. I knew that choice is an illusion cherished by the smaller self and used to momentarily limit the infinite. The Angel of Inspiration arrives from a realm where light is not divided. My friend understood. He had not the illusion of choice — for him, the book was already begun. I understood, then, many secrets of discipleship.

My friend and teacher was smiling at me when I finally noticed my body. His eyes were moist with the sheer radiance of the moment, and though he did not say so, I could see that he was deeply touched to not be alone in the visitation of the Angel. I felt a sense of what it was like for him to live in the depth of the ocean, how lonely it was to live amongst men. And yet, what a companionship it was when the relative world finally leapt to experience the ocean! All this I experienced in a pure moment of Rahim, of compassion.

"Now you know why I must write," he said to me, clasping my hands as he spoke. His steady eyes poured out an infinite tenderness. "Our bodies are dwelling places. We have a sacred duty to summon the Angel. My words are nothing more than food for the Angel. It is Allah's way of speaking the world into wholeness."

We both fell silent, savoring the moment. The smell of our morning meal filled us as the sun warmed our faces. The unspoken words of his new book, the one which became as well known as any of his, danced in the silence between us. I knew that as he summoned each prophet to the altar of his imagination, he would be helping to right the world. For the wisdom of each prophet was a voice of understanding that became a river back to Allah.

"It is not about the knowledge; it is not about the ideas. It is so that the Angel of Inspiration has a home in which to dwell here upon the Earth. Each time we make such a dwelling place, all of creation remembers its purpose. What greater gift can we give?"

14

COMING HOME TO COHERENCE

POWDER SNOW was my earliest introduction to coherence. I was playing outside after a storm; the sun was out, and ice crystals were catching millions of facets of light from the heavens. I dipped my hand and threw a handful of powder into the air. Snowflakes glittered like fairy dust. Something about the light-illuminated snow crystals shimmering against the deep blue sky broke me open. I felt a physical sensation of heat around my heart and pressure rising from my chest. It felt like millions of tiny fingers were tickling the entire inside of my body, so intense was the feeling. It was as if a waterfall of delight were pouring through me. The beauty of the day opened me up and I was in bliss. At that moment I was in a state of coherence with myself, with the world, and with the subtle source of the bliss.

The word "coherence" comes from a Latin root meaning, "to stick together." Its dictionary definition is worth noting: "A cleaving together; an agreement of ideas; consistency; to adhere, to be attached physically, or by affection or some other tie." Coherence, then, is the cleaving together of the parts into a whole.[1]

But there is a built-in contradiction in the definition of the word "coherence." The word "cleave" means to put together; its can also mean "to rend apart; to penetrate or pass through; to separate or sever; to divide into groups having opposing views.

"Coherence" contains within its connotations the notions of both coming together and of differentiating. Not many words embrace two such radically different ideas at the same time. Most of us would likely agree that our society reflects the same dichotomy; we need only look at war to see it highlighted. In war people of one group cooperate (cleave together) and try to destroy (cleave apart) people of another group. But war is not the only activity that defines us. Within the broader context of culture the multiple problems facing our world underscore the need for us to stick together. Yet the primacy of the individual is nearly a religion in the West — never before have the potentials for individuation been as great. What are we to do?

I believe we must join together and learn to direct our powers wisely if we and our planet are to survive. We are disturbing an entire planetary system — a truly remarkable reflection of the power of an individual species. (You cannot view the Earth from space without seeing humanity's signature upon it.) Every invention and technological device that has given us the capacity to affect global systems began as a vibrating idea or an intuitive feeling in the heart and mind of some human being. What is the source of these ideas? Where do these inventions come from? Unless we begin to access a wisdom that is equal to the power of our inventions, we are playing with a fire that could destroy the world. The accessing of this wisdom is an act of coherence; it is a gathering together of the pieces and parts of our experience rewoven into a whole within our own hearts and minds.

From the mysterious dance of quantum fluctuations to the movement of galactic clusters, the entire spectrum of creation appears to be an endlessly recurring system of fluctuating processes. Like an incoming tide bathing the dancing cilia of a sea anemone, harmonized changes cascade throughout the cosmos, linking its constituent bits in a reciprocal (and possibly evolving) relationship and creating the standing waves of order and structure that are the substance of our bodies and of all worlds. The cosmos may be a single relational gesture, a coherent body in the process of becoming known to itself.

A particular kind of cloud formation is my favorite illustration of the concept of standing waves. Just to the west of Boulder, Colorado, clouds that resemble long, thin dragons form on the lee of the Rocky Mountains. In time-lapse images, you can see the dynamic dance of the clouds as the winds move through them. The clouds hold their form even though it is clear that the atmosphere within them is constantly streaming through them. They maintain coherence in the midst of change. Like those clouds, when our bodies stay within certain narrow parameters at basic levels such as temperature, acid-alkaline balance, and electrical potential, we maintain a standing wave of form in the midst of change. It may be that everything we know in the material universe is made up of standing waves of radiation collected in self-organizing local conditions — we affectionately call some of them planets and stars.

Coherence is the cleaving together of individual parts in the midst of change. Coherence can appear in any collection that maintains integrity and yet is responsive and available to the flow of a greater energy through it. If we turn our attention to nature we find numerous examples of coherence in action. On a recent trip here in Alaska, I came up to a small island where hundreds of birds were perched. As the boat neared the shoreline, the birds rose together and began to skim the water, flying inches apart and turning instantaneously as a group. And I have seen fish display the same grouping phenomenon as their concerted motion ripples through a school like a contracting muscle. Multiple individual members come together and, for a time, form a single coherent body.

Another powerful example of coherence in nature can be found in the fractal quality of the natural landscape. Fractals are patterns of organization that repeat across a broad scale of size. When you look out upon the forested ridges that lead to a distant mountain range, you are looking at a fractal landscape. The shape of individual needle arrays are repeated in the shape of the trees, found in the undulations of water-eroded hillsides, and finally repeated in the mountains themselves. The repetition of similar fractal shapes creates a coherent visual landscape that is enormously pleasing to the human eye and heart. We enjoy being witnesses to coherence because it awakens within us a sense of reverence and awe.

Hurricanes are one of the most dramatic examples of coherence in nature. (Though they have a powerful destructive potential, hurricanes are also extremely beautiful, and we see their elegant spiral shape repeated at a larger scale in the formation of galaxies.) They begin as a wrinkle in the eastward-flowing trade winds, and self-organize through a complex process of heat transfer. Heat from the ocean (known as sensible heat) warms a body of air, which rises. As the air is rising moisture evaporates from the surface of the ocean, carrying with it latent heat. At higher altitudes the warm, moist air cools; water condenses out, and the latent heat is released, increasing the temperature of the air column. (The central air column can rise as high as 50 thousand feet before dissipating into the atmosphere.)

The rising air creates a low-pressure area that, at a certain point, begins to rotate — slowly at first and then faster as the conservation of angular momentum increases its spin. (Skaters use the same principle when they pull their arms in toward their bodies to increase the rate of their spins.) The temperature gradient between the central column and the condensing clouds that spiral around the center creates the violence of the storms. Some of the heat that is carried upward sinks back down, compressing and heating the central column and producing the eerie clear skies in the eye of the hurricane. The rates of evaporation and heat transfer increase, and the storm system becomes self-organizing and self-sustaining — sometimes covering hundreds of miles of ocean.

Technically, hurricanes are described as self-organizing, non-equilibrium systems. The following definition of a self-organizing, non-equilibrium system comes from an elegant work by Lee Smolin called *The Life of the Cosmos:*

A distinguishable collection of matter, with recognizable boundaries which has a flow of energy, and possibly matter, passing through it, while maintaining, for time scales long compared to the dynamical times scales of its internal processes, a stable configuration far from thermodynamic equilibrium. This configuration is maintained by the action of cycles involving the transport of matter and energy within the system and between the system and its exterior. Further, the system is stabilized against small perturbations by the existence of feedback loops which regulate the rates of flow of the cycles.[2]

Smolin's definition of a self-organizing, non-equilibrium system, though written in technical language, parallels the definition of the word "coherence": he is talking about the tendency of body to stay together. His definition also highlights the relationship between the system and its context: integrity of the system is maintained only through multiple exchanges with what is exterior to the system. In other words, the system is integrally linked to its larger environment. We have already seen that hurricanes meet the basic requirement of this definition. So do many other systems, including living beings. In other words, the self-organizing, non-equilibrium capacities of the universe are the primary sources of coherence.

Smolin's definition also points out that overall coherence depends on a certain amount of imbalance. There must be enough imbalance in the system to set up a need for exchange with a larger environment. How does this translate into our personal lives? It means that we need to be slightly askew in order to interact with the universe. This is extremely bad news for the control freaks that live within us. No matter how hard we try to maintain equilibrium, the very nature of self-organizing systems will continually push us toward some kind of imbalance to maintain the energy flow necessary for life.

At one time I gave classes on the creative process, assisting individuals to gain better access to their creativity. There was a painter in the class whose technical skills were far beyond those of the rest of the class, though her creative process in other aspects of her life (particularly with men) was, to put it kindly, problematic. The very control and attention to detail that gave her technical proficiency in her painting sabotaged her freedom and spontaneity.

I asked her to make messy drawings, to purposefully create images that were chaotic and lacking in order. After months of foot-dragging she finally brought her work to class, sketch pad clutched to her chest as if protecting her heart. She let out a shriek when she realized that the very drawing she had not wanted to show us was folded over in plain view of the whole class. Freudian slips, glitches, mistakes, and accidents are all tender emissaries from the universe reminding us that a certain amount of imbalance is necessary for maintaining the coherence of living systems.

As Smolin points out, the configuration of self-organizing systems is maintained by the action of cycles. When I was young, my father brought home a motorized gyroscope from his work. It was small enough for me to hold it in my hands. When the motor was switched on, the spinning weight that was mounted on the shaft created its gyroscopic action. That machine seemed to have a mind of its own. If I attempted to shift it out of its position, it would fight me. The spinning created a stable platform that resisted change — a principle that is used in the guidance system of rockets and found on a grander scale in planetary rotation. Spinning creates stability. The completion of cycles creates coherence.

Nearly every system we can imagine — from a human body to a galactic cluster — is subject to cyclical processes. The time frame of these cycles varies from nanoseconds at the atomic level to billions of years at the level of the evolution of the universe. Every part of our natural world is a function of nested cycles; conversely, the coherence of any system is intimately connected to the cyclical nature of our universe.

Our search for coherence is the search for invariant constants, for the standing waves of truth. Achieving coherence is a lifetime process that depends on attention, discipline, heartfelt intuition, and freedom. And we need to stay alert. Much of what we take to be coherence can turn out to be mere habit and adaptation to chronic areas of imbalance. We are always aligned with some attractor in our lives. Indeed, we could not function without such structure. The task of true inquiry, of being curious and alive as human beings, is to explore the depth of those alignments as we foster ties with greater patterns.

The desire to connect to the heart of reality is at the heart of human experience. The key to attaining personal coherence is to find those aspects of your life that resonate most deeply for you. If your heart is burdened with sadness and grief, then those layers must be worked through. Old material and constraints imposed by family, culture, and life trauma must be released while the creative action of new expression is nurtured. The act of finding coherence is an equal part shedding and building of our inner lives.

Underneath the turbulence of our times is an invitation to join in the coherence of the cosmos. Only we can answer this call. No one else — no teacher, no teaching, no system of knowledge or blind belief — will bring it. It is ours to do. And we are capable. We approach coherence when we discover the subtle organizing patterns of the universe and come into resonant relationship with them. We approach it when we reach into the difficult fires of our relationships and conflicts and find the places where we can cleave together. We approach it when we rise with passion to greet the beauty of each dawn, and when our hearts are set aflame with the desire to return something to the universe that has given us so much. As we attune to the rhythms, patterns, and heartbeats of the cosmos our estrangement from our bodies, ecosystem, cultures, and souls will soften. We shall finally come home.

Notes

1. See *New Webster's Dictionary of the English Language,* (Delair, 1971).
2. See Lee Smolin, *The Life of the Cosmos,* (Oxford University Press, 1997), p. 155.

Additional Resources

INTERNET LINKS

http://128.187.18.132/C13A1a.html
An animation of a standing wave.

http://www.worldhurricanes.com/
A good introductory site for information on hurricanes.

http://www.glenbrook.k12.il.us/gbssci/phys/Class/waves/u10l4b.html
A tutorial on standing waves by Tom Henderson of Glenbrook South High School.

http://www.aoml.noaa.gov/hrd/
National Oceanic and Atmospheric Administration's hurricane site. This site is a source of scientific research into hurricanes and their formation.

http://algodones.unm.edu/~ehdecker/SOS/SOS.html
A tutorial on self-organizing systems by Ethan H. Decker; Department of Biology, University of New Mexico, Albuquerque, NM.

http://www.brint.com/Systems.htm
Extensive links to complex systems theory and practice.

http://www.c3.lanl.gov/~rocha/sa2.html
A very technical paper on how self-organizing systems function around symbolic formation.

BOOKS

Childre, Doc, author; and Bruce Cryer, translator. *From Chaos to Coherence: Advancing Emotional and Organizational Intelligence Through Inner Quality Management.* Butterworth-Heinemann, 1998. ISBN 075067007X

Linde, Charlotte. *Life Stories: The Creation of Coherence.* Oxford University Press, 1993. ISBN 0195073738

Mir, Mustansir. *Coherence in the Qur'an.* American Trust Publications, 1987. ISBN 0892590653

Pokorny, Jiri and Tsu-Ming Wu. *Biophysical Aspects of Coherence and Biological Order.* Springer Verlag, 1998. ISBN 3540646515

Smolin, Lee. *The Life of the Cosmos*. Oxford University Press, 1997. ISBN 019510837X

Swinburne, Richard. *The Coherence of Theism*. Clarendon Press, 1993. Clarendon Library of Logic and Philosophy. ISBN 0198240694

Interlude

BIRDSONG

*Rumi, a Persian poet of the thirteenth century, was a
conventionally accomplished cleric and scholar who lived in
what is now Konya, Turkey. One day in a sugar market he
met a wild dervish, named Shams, who had a powerful
mystical capacity. The moment the two met Rumi's life
changed forever. The two began mystical conversations that
lasted until Shams's death a few short years later.
Rumi spontaneously created rhymed couplets that embodied
difficult metaphysical truths in simple,
elegant imagery. It is said that he rarely wrote down what
he created — in fact, he often composed while whirling
(a spiritual practice that he is credited with beginning).
His access to truth and his capacity to cloak it in such
beauty and tenderness speaks volumes about the power
of his heart and, perhaps, accounts for the fact that
currently Rumi has the distinction of being the most read
poet in the world.*

In the spring the birds are everywhere. They take to
the sky from the distant marshes and the morning is often
made over with birdsong. That morning was no exception.

I heard the laughter before I saw the two men round the path along the creekbed where I was walking. If there were birdsong in the human heart, which I sometimes swear there is, it would sound something like their laughter.

Most laughter is a release — a venting of some burden. Most laughter has an object, a mirror that reflects the longing in a heart for freedom. Not this laughter. Not this morning. This was a laughter of fullness that greeted me. Full of joy, with no cloud of misery.

As the two came near, I saw that their eyes were closed. They were walking blind, and their laughter amid the flowers was a wing of finely-feathered joy that lifted them into some other realm.

Love has no object if it is truly love. This I saw that morning, for there was no "other" in the gesture that these two made of their lives. They trusted each other to see and yet they were both walking blind. I would not place such trust in any man or woman. But then I had a heart that had not melted before the sun of such union.

Our beloved teacher opened his eyes first. He must have sensed my presence — though they both seemed aware of worlds that could not be seen. He smiled at me. I have never seen a human being so grateful to be alive. There was no armor, no shield, no weapon of ill-advised thought in that smile. There was only the ascending curve of gratitude that carried with it the birdsong, the flowers, the morning, and the promise of the golden sky above us.

It was then that I understood that gratitude is the doorway to the fire we call love.

My eyes welled up as I looked into his. The thousand places in which I resented the life I was called to live stood before the light of his gaze, and suddenly I knew why it was that I could not truly hear the birdsong I had been listening to all that morning's walk. I had not been listening with gratitude.

The veils of resentment were lifted from my heart, and I knew why birds sing every morning. They are, and always will be, grateful for the light. So grateful that they cannot stop the sound that leaps up from their hearts. A blessing is bestowed upon our world whenever love has found wings.

It was then that Shams opened his eyes. A desert wildness lived behind those darkened orbs. I saw the stars spinning in the heavens. I saw within him a fiery presence of enormous radiance. And I saw that love is born of such fire.

I think it is not possible to be in love and stay tied to the donkey of judgment. I had heard all the gossip about the two.

Who had not? It was the talk of town. And I, too, must confess that I had formed my heart into certain shapes when this wild dervish had appeared in the life of our beloved teacher.

But there, in the flowered morning of my awakening, I was stripped of all judgment. The purity of their laughter and the gracious invitation to gratitude that was in their eyes informed me a deep well of love had appeared in our midst. Such love takes down the veils of pretense.

I was made naked that morning by the rich and sonorous chords of laughter that was pure freedom in the making. Only a heart that has been made new by love could find the innocence to laugh in such a way.

The two passed and I was left with the rushing wings of dawn and strand upon strand of birdsong that wove itself up into a rich, thick carpet of beauty.

Chapter Fifteen

A Matter of the Heart

THE MYSTICAL PROCESS unfolds in a well-chronicled sequence of experiences. After an initial awakening and an intuition of contact with a deeper realm of reality, the mystic begins a trial in which he or she is faced with difficulties and disturbances. The recognition that such forces exist crosses all cultural boundaries: the Lakota Sioux have a concept that they call "The Bad Holy(ies)" — their name for eruptions of violence, disturbances, or discord and for events such as the Holocaust. St. Catherine of Sienna spent her teenage years praying in her bedroom and was often beset by intense visual images of the darkest elements of her society. Tibetan Buddhist students are asked to intentionally visualize wrathful, vengeful deities in order to strengthen themselves by facing the darkest components of their own internal worlds. St. John of the Cross called his descent into meaninglessness, confusion, and disturbance " the dark night of the soul."

The intensified weather patterns, disease migrations, biological terrorism, proliferating weapons, cultural upheavals, wealth imbalances, and other global dislocations that we are seeing are portals of emergence. For cultures as for individuals the emergence of these forces — in all their difficult and disruptive aspects — invites us to consider the totality of life and to reach beyond our cherished beliefs and assumptions to develop new understanding and insight into our human condition. Indeed, Jungian psychologists would say that we need to integrate our cultural shadow material if we are ever to fully mature.

Our genius for invention and discovery wreaks havoc on the planet when we lose touch with the web of relationships that sustain the world; knowledge is sundered from wisdom. Consider the root meaning of the word genius: it comes from Latin, means "tutelary spirit," and originally was associated with a male form of generative energy. (The Greek prefix *gen*, associated with birth and the Sanskrit *jan*, meaning "to beget, bear or produce," are also associated with the word.) The *daimon* of the Greeks was translated into Latin as *genii* (or *jinni*). And it is necessary to explore the notion of the daimonic if we are to understand where genius has become disconnected from its capacity to support life, since genius stripped of heart becomes demonic.

The Greeks understood the *daimon* as the power that flows through the lover, the poet, and the artist, as well as that which supports leadership and religious impulse. Plato argued that it was a form of divine madness that would consume people. Socrates described his own *daimon* thusly: "This sign, which is a kind of voice, first began to come to me when I was a child."

Basic tendencies and capacities that appear early in a person's life often reappear later as life choices, callings, or vocations. (Remember Nikola Tesla's announcement that he would power the world from Niagara Falls?) These intangible qualities, more powerful than familial and cultural conditioning, are part of the basic matrix of each human being — an encoding unique to each individual. And like the sun, wind, and gravity they simply are. Individuals determine if and how their unique capacities are used, depending on their response to life's invitation.

We each have a soul signature — a "unique pattern of sensibilities and powers"— that constitutes our relation to the cosmos.[1] We each have a daimon. The successful assimilation of the *daimon* seeds the gifts of humanity; its distortion creates dictators, despots, and tyrants. When the Prophet Mohammed first began to hear the voice of the Koran coming to him, he confided to his beloved companion Kajidha that he was afraid he was being possessed by *Jinns*. The *daimon* of his life turned out to not be some shadowy spirit, but a cosmic revelation upon which an entire religion and civilization was built. Hitler, blinded by gas in the trenches of World War I, made a bargain with the universe. He said that if his eyesight were restored he would go on to restore the glory of Germany. He became captured by the demonic. (In films of Hitler you can see the possession occur bodily as he tentatively walks toward the podium and suddenly becomes electrified by an energy that ignites into malevolence and hatred.)

True navigators learn to know their *daimons*. By purifying the tendencies of their personality distortions, they become transparent windows to the fundamental power of creation. They integrate both the generative and the guiding functions of the daimonic. Our work, the great common work, is the transmutation of self into the abiding power of generation. All mystics, saints, and prophets have participated in some way in this process. And each one of us is, in our way, also participating. Our heartfelt yearning for something greater supports us in the transformation.

The yearning for something greater than ourselves has many names in many cultures: the Greeks named this function Eros. Eros was one of the four original gods. Chaos, Gaea (Mother Earth), and Tartarus (dark pit of Hades) were the other three characters in the original mandala of creation. (In the language of chaos theory, Eros is the strange attractor that brings coherence to the other forces of nature.) The interplay of the world — the void, chaos, and longing — created the world. Eros (longing), seized life-giving arrows, pierced Gaea's (the world's) cold bosom, and produced the fecund greenery of life. The longing for life brings fullness to the world. The fullness of life is waiting to find a more complete expression through humanity. Each one of us can unfold this potential if we are willing to be pierced by Eros's arrows — to have our heart opened by the power of life.

In the Sufi tradition the motive power of creation is described as the desire of the Absolute to know Itself. The worlds — both material and immaterial — are merciful expressions of this longing. The exhalation of Allah reverberates throughout the cosmos as a breath of mercy, and upon the wings of this exquisite compassion all of nature takes form. *Himma* activates the seeker's return to wholeness.

Himma is an Arabic word that means, variously, "meditating," "conceiving," "imagining," "projecting," and "ardently desiring." It is also associated with creative intentionality and the summoning of vital force into the heart center. According to Sufi mystic Ibn Arabi, *Himma* is the power that makes imagination possible, allowing individuals direct access to the energy of cosmic formation. When *Himma* is invoked, the veils between the worlds grow thin — it has the power to summon aspects of the cosmos and create real, actual outcomes that are not in the least associated with illusory projections of the psyche.

We touch *Himma*, the generating power of creation, when we are truly alive to the impulses of our hearts. Tesla's burning desire to bring a new invention into being gave the world the alternating current generator. Lewis and Clark's desire to see new lands and explore the unknown allowed them to accomplish the extraordinary and make their way across wilderness. Black Elk's love for his people carried him and those around him through the bleakness of their time, and Queen Elizabeth's marriage to her kingdom transformed a society. Wherever the passion of the true heart is aroused, the course of life is changed. Whether this change is for the better or the worse depends on the purity of each participant. The movement to integration is not a function of the intellect but of a deeply felt shift of the heart.

As we dive deeply into the heart of matter, we are discovering the vast fields of energy that are linked in a reciprocal relationship with the rest of the universe. And we humans are part of those relationships: the human heart beats its rhythm alongside the pulsing vibration of stars. Our purpose as human beings is to make the coherence of the universe explicit as a conscious experience.

Many indigenous cultures evolved ways to directly perceive and respond to the fields of life in ways that optimized coherence and connection and de-emphasized the individual. Western experience, on the other hand, has been a centuries-long experiment in coming to understand the function of an individuated consciousness. The foundation of objectivity upon which the scientific method has been built presupposes a stable, differentiated point of view or reference point from which reality can be tested. Westerners must face the prospect that a society based on the primacy of the individual may spin the world into destruction because we have little ability to relate in meaningful ways with the whole. With the advent of the quantum revolution and the emergence of chaos theory, though, Western science is having to consider that relative relations are as important in the functioning of the universe as is objective knowledge.

We are being challenged to enter into a new relationship with the world. This new relationship marries the whole-field relationships of indigenous cultures to the success of Western scientific and technological achievements, and is anchored in spiritual understanding. A culture built upon an expanding ethic of whole-field awareness is able to introduce coherence and bring about a merging of the inner spiritual intuition with the outer context of our environment. The heart is the pivot upon which this synthesis turns. Simple proficiency in a task is not, in itself, going to determine whole-field coherence. As the seat of intuition, an open heart is aware of the world and acts with the sensitivity that such awareness engenders.

Recent research suggests that the heart is an organ of intelligence.[2] During our development in the womb the heart literally migrates to its final position. A membrane forms which descends through the brain and takes up its position in the chest cavity. The heart has its own neural system — its own brain — made up of complex ganglia (neural nets) that send, receive, and sort information. The ganglia are connected to information-gathering sensors within the heart that feed, via the vagus nerve, to the brain. The heart is also a gland — releasing a hormone that affects blood vessels, kidneys, the adrenal glands, and many of the regulatory regions of the brain.

Research at Heartmath (an innovative institute devoted to helping develop heart coherence) has shown that when we are within a few feet of each other our hearts come into sympathetic vibration with the nervous systems of other people. As we have learned, sympathetic resonance is one of the primary modes of energy exchange in the universe. And so it is with our hearts. We can live without breath for a period of time; we can live without food, water, or other forms of nourishment for indefinite periods, but when the heart stops death is immediate.

Many spiritual traditions speak of the highest wisdom residing in the heart. Ramana Maharshi, one of the spiritual giants of the twentieth century, spoke of the seat of the self as being on the right side of the heart. According to Ramana, when we dwell in the heart we have reached the end of our spiritual journey. And a very revered yogi in India, around whom many miracles were said to have manifested, once said, "The heart is the hub of the universe, go there and wander."[3] He meant this quite literally: in deep meditative states, the heart is said to function as a gateway to a direct experience of other planes of existence.

The enormous challenges of our modern world will be met if enough hearts are aroused. Can we design a commerce of the heart? And what does the architecture of caring look like? Understanding the physiology of our emotions can help us to see the world as it is actually unfolding and not how we have been imprinted to see it. The amygdala, a small almond-shaped structure in the mid-brain, shapes our immediate emotional responses based on information assembled from our early life experiences. We need to recognize the sway our early programming has on our present actions and reactions and use the tools of conscious attention to repattern our responses. When we do correct self-limiting habits of thought, we are liberated and can allow ourselves to become vulnerable, sensitive, and aware of the world.

Understanding helps us to discern the patterns of an event and to release our confusion and disorientation. We trust more often when we understand, and we understand better when we trust; this is a reciprocal relationship between the heart and the head. As we develop whole-field awareness and greater pattern recognition we can orient ourselves more easily and respond in heartfelt ways.

Forgiveness seems to be critical to the opening of the heart. We have all had experiences that have closed our hearts and wounded our capacity to care. We cannot control the wounding, but we can choose to forgive.

Extending kindness toward others encourages the movement of heart into the world. Our heart's impulses can lead us to an ever-deepening relationship with the self and the people with whom we interact. When we invite our hearts to meet the heart of the world, we release its intuitive wisdom.

Recalling heart-opening moments can settle us and return us to a state of coherence. A daily review of events, with a focus on those moments when we felt appreciation, gratitude, or compassion can ground us and remind us of the wisdom and spaciousness of love.

Immersion in beauty helps to cultivate an open heart. A simple contemplation of beauty can soothe and inspire, lifting our moods and strengthening our sense of well-being. Fortunately, nature provides an ever-changing tapestry of beauty that relaxes the heart and helps us remember our relationship to the greater patterns of life.

Some form of prayer or an appeal to a force greater than ours can help us surrender our egos. Some form of surrender is essential for the opening of the heart and has practical applications as well: we cannot change situations or solve problems unless we are willing to give up our attachment to outcomes and allow entry to the unexpected and unanticipated.

A steady diet of creative activity — both inner and outer — feeds the heart. As we dare to imagine into our soul's depth, we go beyond the normal content of the mind and into the creative fire of inner vision.

How best can each of us access our own heart and its wisdom? We can draw upon the whole-field awareness known by our ancestors. We can learn to engineer a technological world to support that awareness. We can release the fundamental core of spiritual knowing from the encrustations of dogma. We can develop our personal capacities for empathy and understanding that are necessary to support sensitivity to many worlds at the same time. We can seek our role within the larger cycles of the universe. We can come into coherence with the heart of matter, and take our place as mediators of wisdom, insight, and courage. It is a matter of navigating from the heart.

Notes

1. See Rollo May, *Love and Will*, 1st ed. (Norton, 1969).

2. HeartMath Research Center, 14700 West Park Avenue, Boulder Creek, CA 95006.

3. This quotation is attributed to Swami Nityananda. See his Chidakash Gita at http://www.ns.sympatico.ca/umbada/mcgl.htm.

Additional Resources

BOOKS

Almaas, A. H., *Essence: The Diamond Approach to Inner Realization*. Diamond Books, 1990. ISBN 0877286272

————. *Facets of Unity: The Enneagram of Holy Ideas*. Diamond Books, 1998. ISBN 0936713143

Kornfield, Jack. *A Path With Heart: A Guide Through the Perils and Promises of Spiritual Life*. Bantam Doubleday Dell, 1993. ISBN 0553372114

Pearsall, Paul. *The Heart's Code*. Broadway Books, 1998. ISBN 0767900774

Soygal, Rinpoche. *The Tibetan Book of Living and Dying*. Harper San Francisco, 1992. ISBN 0062507931

Lovers are not to be helped with advice.
Love's current cannot be stood against.
The intellect fails
to understand the intoxicated one.

Even the threshold of entry
of the one who has left himself
confuses the wise.

The fragrance of love
found amidst the gathering of the heart
is a wine
that topples kings.

Life freezes without the embrace of the soul.
The journey becomes troubled
and the body loses its luster.

If the heavens were not in love,
If the stars were not intoxicated by the
heart's embrace,
all the whirling would stop.
The celestial lights would cry,
"Enough, how long must we spin?"

The reed-flute universe
is filled with the breath of the creation.
Stillness is the thunder of discontent.

Oh soul! Climb to the night sky's roof
And create chaos with your song!

— Jalalludin Rumi
(Translated and adapted by the author
from Kulliyat-i Shams, v.535)

To truly care for the world is to come into deep relationship with it. Eight hundred years ago the Persian mystic and poet, Jalalludin Rumi, ascribed motive power to the whirling energy of love. His poem asks us to consider the reality and breadth of that power and our response to it. Yes, it is a daunting task in this time of rapid global change. Yes, it is easier to love those with whom we feel safe, and even then it is difficult. Yet the demand of the heart is for relationship. And a truly open heart is able to come into relationship with all beings, wherever and whatever they may be doing.

Love is the force that sets the heavens spinning and keeps our world turning. It creates coherence and completes cycles. Love sustains the courageous actions of those who work for peace and empowers us to meet the world with compassion. Love liberates. It inspires an inventor to labor for years on an invention before it comes to fruition and gives parents the patience to support their children through years of growing up. We are participating in an unfolding universe, and each one of us helps to determine its form.

Each act we perform, each thought we think, and each feeling we hold in our hearts is inextricably woven into the fabric of the world around us.

We have heard many stories throughout this book; each one has helped illuminate a single common thread. The sacred thread that weaves together the observational skills of a scientist, the dedication of an inventor, the soul of a philosopher, the passion of a social reformer, and the spirit of a mystic is the power of an awakened heart. Whenever the passion of the true heart is summoned, the course of life is changed. Wisdom flows through the myriad processes of our world. As we awaken we will hear the heart of a wise planet. Unraveling the mystery of that wisdom is the art of our lives, the hope for our future, and our gift to generations yet to come.

About the Author

Because his father was a glaciologist, David LaChapelle grew up next to glaciers and mountain peaks. The impact of nature's beauty was such that his heart would literally soar and he would find himself singing songs to the world. This was his early initiation into telling the story of the world — an initiation that heightened his intuitive capacities.

And because his mother was a writer, an "information fountain" with a passion for intellectual and spiritual concerns, David's intuitive capacity turned naturally and easily to the spiritual traditions of the planet. The evolution of the Earth provided a conscious and spiritual backdrop for his own radical connection to nature.

Writing poetry, plays, poems, essays and voluminous letters as a youth, as well as reading through the great works in the English language, acquainted him first hand with the creative process. With teenage years played out amidst the psychedelic revolution in the Haight Ashbury district of San Francisco, he explored Eastern religions, taking to heart the many tales of the search for enlightenment, the search for the sacred.

Along the way he studied energy healing, bodywork, many aspects of yoga, gestalt therapy and other disciplines of personal transformation. All of this remained mere technique until he met John Fire Lame Deer, a Lakota Medicine man who opened for him a whole world view and sensibility. Next came a visit to an ashram in India, with exposure to the philosophy and practice of Kundalini yoga.

Back in the U.S., he taught skiing to children for three years, and then joined a Holistic Health Clinic in Boulder, Colorado, working with individuals and groups to investigate many aspects of the spiritual path. Also leading Wilderness Quests, he helped deepen people's inner connections. A move to Alaska launched his writing career where the remarkable purity of Alaska was the inspiration for both further inner work, and the process of organizing and systematizing his philosophical insights.

See www.tidesofchange.org

If you have enjoyed *Navigating the Tides of Change*,
you might also enjoy other

BOOKS TO BUILD A NEW SOCIETY

New Society Publishers' mission is to publish books that
contribute in fundamental ways to building an ecologically sustainable
and just society, and to do so with the least possible impact on the
environment, in a manner that models this vision.

Our books provide positive solutions for people
who want to make a difference.
We specialize in:

Sustainable Living

Ecological Design and Planning

Natural Building & Appropriate Technology

Environment and Justice

New Forestry

Conscientious Commerce

Resistance and Community

Nonviolence

Progressive Leadership

Educational and Parenting Resources

For a full list of NSP's titles, please call 1-800-567-6772
or check out our web site at:
www.newsociety.com

NEW SOCIETY PUBLISHERS